MW00478908

The

Witch's

Cloak

A Memoir of the Unseen

The Witch's Cloak

A Memoir of the Unseen

Adriene Nicastro

Pathways to Freedom Press
Bellefonte, Pennsylvania

The Witch's Cloak: A Memoir of the Unseen

Copyright © 2021 by Adriene Nicastro
All rights reserved.

Original cover photograph
Pixabay-celtic-woman-welsh-scottish-female-3122253

Cover design © 2021 by Adriene Nicastro

No part of this book may be reproduced or transmitted in any manner whatsoever without the express written permission of the publisher except for the use of brief quotations in critical articles and book reviews.

Most names and identifying details have been changed to protect individuals' privacy.

Pathways to Freedom Press
Bellefonte, PA
www.pathwaystofreedom.com

Library of Congress: 2020918875

ISBN:
        Paperback 978-1-7358558-3-7

Acknowledgements

Love and gratitude to all those who made this book possible including my family, friends, clients, students, teachers, angels, guides, spirit, and last but never least, Divine Flame and my Higher Self.

This book is dedicated to my children, who chose me as a vessel and caretaker for their journey here. Your wisdom and courage leave me in awe. Thank you for enduring the many experiments and dissertations on spiritual topics du jour, for helping me to grow into a better mom, and for molding me into a more powerful healer.

This work is also dedicated to my small but potent coven, otherwise known as "sisters from different misters":

To Marta, for reminding me what sisterhood is, letting me witness and be part of your unending dedication to Spirit, countless hours of processing our path, and sharing your profoundly radiant soul;

To Nancy, for your refreshing and candid friendship, loyalty, and loving support of my journey;

To Melissa, for your kindness, overwhelming generosity, and infectious sense of humor;

To Tehmina, for your intuition, your sisterhood in awakening, and believing in my abilities;

To Debbie, for your infinite sweetness, generosity, and genuine kindness;

And finally, to Tia, for nearly thirty years of ups and downs, your mischievously contagious laugh, and for our shared love of human evolution.

Table of Contents

Dear Reader

Do you believe?

In what, you ask?

In the unseen, of course.

If you're not sure, but seek answers...

If you desire confirmation that you're not alone in your beliefs and/or experiences...

If you want company on your journey...

Welcome to *The Witch's Cloak: A Memoir of the Unseen*, a magical collection of personal accounts with many layers and aspects of life beyond our five senses - stories about manifesting, the angelic world, synchronicity, reincarnation, spirit communication, and more. Woven into an inspirational and unique memoir of discovery and sacred awakening, *The Witch's Cloak* holds precious treasures adorned with the jewels of wisdom, gratitude, and profound love. All that's recanted here - the embarrassing bloopers, profound lessons, and heartwarming triumphs - are met with whimsy, candor, humor, and authenticity.

I built my trust in Source, myself, and my Self through years of deeply impactful and highly personal happenings, which gave birth to *The Witch's Cloak*. Within these pages, detailed in each chapter, are my experiences of learning, growing, and living in tune (and at times out of sync) with the unseen, namely spirit, Spirit, Source, and the mystical forces within and all around us. Frequently, however, experiences can remain just that – solely ours: mysterious events, coded within feelings, meant to be lived rather than bound to less-than-perfect words. Therefore, I endeavor to impart my stories by speaking through the heart, a cosmic synthesis of universal tongue. Perhaps, for a moment, I can bring you into my world, and as you step through the doorway, that glimpse may curiously awaken something in you – a memory, an Essence. Hopefully, what calls to you is a love so profound that you'll come inside for a while. And as you enter *The Witch's Cloak's* brief snapshots in time, as your relationship with characters and events unfolds, each story can become uniquely yours. Most of all, I hope it reminds you, dear reader, that the profound exists in our everyday lives, brought to the fore by observation, focus, and a willingness to discover beauty and sacredness moment by moment.

However you navigate *The Witch's Cloak*, may it offer many opportunities to inform and spark thought-provoking contemplation and meaningful discussions. As an aid in this endeavor, chapters conclude with specific reflections, encouraging you to ponder individually, speak with friends and family, or engage with other groups to dialogue and consider the ways each story resonates, challenges, or inspires you.

I wish I could impart all the unusual, wonderful, and mystical events in my life. There have been so many. For now, I offer what's chronicled here. So, cheers to enjoying your journey within and beyond these pages. May what you read spark your own connection to All-that-is, trust in your intuition, a desire to seek answers, and unity with the Cosmos, uniquely yours. And always, may you go forth with many beautiful blessings, discovering heart-warming gifts from the unseen for years to come.

Namaste,

Adriene

Setting the Record Straight

Double, double toil and trouble:
Fire burn and cauldron bubble.
— W. Shakespeare

ecause of this book's title and content, the information to follow serves to help you, dear reader, ponder and digest some valuable morsels on healers, witches, and other supposed "malfeasants." Rather than provide a comprehensive history or narrative on the topic, I intend to clear the way – to disconnect evil and negativity from hearts and minds toward healers, witches, and any seemingly related craft. So, this chapter provides a chance to get up close and personal with your attitudes about the topic before navigating the stories and accounts held within *The Witch's Cloak*.

Before we begin, I ask where you stand on witches, oracles, midwifery, herbalism, and the like?

What are your thoughts and current understanding of them?

What remnants of fear or concern surface as you stand on the precipice of this great adventure – *The Witch's Cloak?*

Let's find out.

There has been much mystery, intrigue, and misinformation around witches and other related healing arts. Devil spawn. Lucifer's concubine. These are just some of the associations grown throughout the centuries, born of fear and mistrust. Unfortunately, fairy tales, folklore, history, and Hollywood have all contributed to a negative image of witches. Still, the damaging impact of these sources remains unmatched to church-created hysteria, as you'll soon discover or may already know. On the other hand, in the last two decades, more interest in alternative wellness, unconventional treatment, and New Age practices have paved the way, leading to broader acceptance.

What does it mean to be a witch? Well, the term encompasses many healing approaches that have innate connections, like branches of a tree. Witches and related healing practitioners use many tools, materials, and methods – intuition, psychic reading, direct communication with the otherworld, purposeful manifesting, herbal healing, energy healing, tarot, crystals, and more – to carry out their skills according to their personal intent. Use your imagination because this kind of healing encompasses a wide swath of possibilities. However, practicing any of these spiritual tools doesn't necessarily make one a witch, any more than using all of them does.

Yes, witch, healer, oracle, herbalist, energy worker. Many a label fits under one black pointy hat. I like the term healer, but on many days, calling myself a witch feels just right.

So, who are you?

❖

Long ago, society revered and cherished seers, oracles, and healers for their craft.

In the Middle East, ancient civilizations not only worshipped powerful female deities, but it was often women who practiced the holiest of rituals. Trained in the sacred arts, these priestesses became known as wise women and may have been some of the earliest manifestations of what we now recognize as the witch.

These wise women made house calls, delivered babies, dealt with infertility, and cured impotence. According to Fontaine, "What's interesting about them is that they are so clearly understood to be positive figures in their society. No king could be without their counsel, no army could recover from a defeat without their ritual activity, no baby could be born without their presence."[1]

However, as the mass consciousness became increasingly steeped in fear - especially of the unseen and those dedicated to working with it - being a healer, herbalist, seer, or midwife, bore the risk of being labeled as a

---

[1] *The History of Witches, From Revered Healers to Persecuted Spellcasters*, October 31, 2015/Updated October 13, 2020, allthatsinteresting.com.

practitioner of the dark arts. Eventually, any work with the unseen became synonymous with the term witch.

Much mystery has shrouded the early roots of witches and healers. (And lifetimes of turmoil and persecution have likely compounded the secrecy.) Their long and winding lineage is intimately linked to the first birthing of religion called Druidry – a Paganistic view of Source discovered as early as 25,000 years ago in the caves of western Europe.

Druids, meaning "knowledge of the oak," revered trees and worshipped Mother Earth. They valued and honored Her sacredness as provider, nurturer, and protector. Possessing an advanced knowledge of plant medicine and herbalism, Druids knew how to work with and communicate with floras and manipulate energies for creation. They were scholarly writers, musicians, and poets, and as diviners and oracles, their guidance was highly prized.

Esteemed and sought out for counsel and healing across the ages, Druids fell under suspicion by the masses and suffered great persecution. The most famous period of genocide, attributed to the Romans, caused the Order to nearly disappear by 700-800 AD. (However, their presence grew again through revitalization efforts in Europe that started in the 1800s.)

Eventually, Paganism found its way into medieval Europe. Practices with distinct Druidic roots – herbalism, midwifery, divination, and healing – otherwise known as witchcraft, were primarily performed by women. Sadly, around the 1200s, an evolution of negative attitudes and fear toward these practices progressively came to mirror the unfortunate history of the Druids. This oppression, however, arrived via the church, as clergymen, attempting to control the masses, declared witchcraft heresy during a movement known as The Inquisition. Under the thumb of male-dominated churchdom, terror, misogyny, and toxic patriarchy surged. As society bent to this human-created god of fear, execution and death followed, and witchcraft and the healing arts became targets.

What was once a revered and honored craft – helping others heal, delivering babies, offering guidance and counsel, using herbs to treat disease and promote wellness – witches and those accused of witchcraft became labeled as heretics: operating against God (thus the church) and consorting with the devil.

As fear-based tactics continued to be employed by many well-respected clergymen, a mounting dread of the Bubonic Plague brought additional terror and with it the potent and deadly marriage of superstition and blame. With witchcraft cemented in societies' minds as demonic activity (1300s), countless pointing fingers found a "who" to fault and punish for a disease caused by flea-borne bacteria. One might say the Plague left a trail of destruction in its wake – bodies destroyed by illness and those caught in the aftermath, tortured and killed as Plague-guilty witches.

Then in 1487, after two centuries of condemnation, two German Dominican monks, Heinrich Kramer and Jacob Sprenger, published *The Malleus Maleficarum* (Latin for "The Hammer of Witches"), the most famous medieval treatises on witches. It fueled over two additional centuries of terror. And though *The Malleus Maleficarum* stands as its own kind of malevolence, it's not the only publication that attempted to diminish women through the veil of witchcraft.

During this era, public witch trials (and I'm sure many private executions) demonstrated Europe's fever-pitch paranoia toward witches and the healing arts. This negative energy perpetuated a wave of persecution that eventually crossed oceans and permeated the timeline with decades of torture. For over six hundred years, those accused of being a witch suffered unspeakable torment and loss.

While difficult to pinpoint, the actual death toll for those executed remains an area of disagreement. Tens of thousands, hundreds of thousands, and even nine million women by some accounts demonstrate the wide range of estimates.[2] As such, I leave you to your own research, dear reader, into a history rife with acts carried out in the name of salvation.

Many a foul deed has been done in the name of God.

Despite the years burdened by suspicion, fear, and death, witches have seen a revival through Wicca and modern variations of Traditional Witchcraft. In addition, healing arts have grown in many forms, especially in this New Age of spiritual growth.

With such a tumultuous history, it's no wonder that many of us who have been witches, Druids, healers, herbalists,

---

[2] Austin Cline, "*Persecuting Witches and Witchcraft.*" Learn Religions, June 25, 2019, learnreligions.com/persecuting-witches-and-witchcraft-4123033. And J. Blumberg, "*A Brief History of the Salem Witch Trials,*" Smithsonian Magazine, October 23, 2007, smithsonianmag.com/history/a-brief-history-of-the-salem-witch-trials-175162489.

seers, midwives, and such, in other lifetimes, find a palpable dread that accompanies our desire to pursue our arts, once again. I can even say that as I embarked on publishing *The Witch's Cloak*, an old fear gnawed its way out of my solar plexus – a toothy, decaying worm that threatened to halt years of creative work – trying to keep all that rests within these pages hidden in the shadows.

I won't let it win.

As we leave that savage history behind us, there is one vital aspect of the craft that I'd like to impart, beginning with the most common association of being a witch. In other words, what do you immediately think of when faced with the idea of witches and witchcraft?

If you said magic, then we're on the same page!

Magic and use of the unseen are synonymous in the minds of the many. So, let's set the record straight: We *all* interact with and call the unseen into service in countless ways, like a witch. That is to say...

We all do magic.

While seemingly relegated to the land of fantasy, witches, or other-than-mainstream healing arts, magic is part of our everyday life, a use of the unseen that most people do unconsciously.

How, you ask?

Magic is merely the manipulation of energy, molding the unseen by intention.

Now, I know you may be thinking, "What do you mean? I *don't* do magic!"

Let me elaborate.

Everything is a particular vibration of energy. Everything.

Energy is. It's not good or bad but shaped by the intent we give it.

Our intent determines the nature of any energy; thought creates as we mold mental energy by our emotions and feelings. Emotional energy joins with thought to give our mental energy direction and purpose. How we use energy makes it positive or negative, loving or unloving. The energy used to heal, comfort, and soothe is the same energy used to injure, attack, and destroy. Our intentions create very different outcomes depending on how we shape our personal spiritual energy and release it in our world.[3]

Simply put, every time you set your mind to do something, the movement and effort you put toward that goal – the time, the thought, the love of your creation, process, and direction – is all energy. The energy you require to manifest your desire is *in you* as an intimate part of your being, as well as that which you *call to you* to make your dreams come true.

Yes, you manipulate energy every day.

Let me say again…you do magic. And you do it all the time! We all do magic by using the power of our sacred, God-given Self.

---

[3] Adriene Nicastro, *The Soul-Discovery Journalbook: An Intimate Journey into Self, Volume III,* (Bellefonte, PA: Pathways to Freedom Press, 2021), p. 276.

So, what about witches?

A witch (or healer) is just consciously using energy. They know how to direct their thoughts, feelings, and intentions to get desired outcomes. They call on the power of God in them, around them, and in their healing tools (however they see/experience that Divine Flow) to make manifest their creations and healing endeavors.

If their intentions (or anyone's, for that matter) are for ill-will, that is a personal error in thinking, one they'll have to rebalance through karma and/or forgiveness. Ill-will is not a function of being a witch (or Druid, healer, or seer, for that matter), but a manifestation of a person's beliefs and how they relate to the world. This is the case for everyone. Any of us can misuse energy, manipulating it to do our bidding. We are all capable of negative thinking, lower emotional states, and mean-spirited/destructive acts – a function of having a personality and being a human. But by the Universe's good grace, abuse of energy and employment of free will to a harmful end helps us learn that hurting another has repercussions, especially toward ourselves. Or, as the spiritual law states – What goes around, comes around. Always.

Whether you like it or not, witches are here to stay. They are a consummate archetype and an integral part of the Divine Feminine, giving birth to the New, nurturing life, sustaining through acts that make everything/everyone grow. And whether you realize it or not, Paganistic practices have woven their way into our hearts and homes – decorating Christmas trees, carving jack-o-lanterns, wearing wedding bands, covering our mouths when we yawn, honoring the solstice/change of seasons, putting stars on our homes and candles in our windows. These cherished practices are part of our world and filled with a beautifully rich history.

So, dear reader, call yourself what you like. Witch or not...

You do magic.

You are *more* than magic.

Thank the stars for it!

The Mysterious Gap

*In oneself lies the whole world
and if you know how to look and learn,
the door is there and the key is in your hand.
Nobody on earth can give you either
the key or the door to open, except yourself.*
~Jiddu Krishnamurti

I've spent years seeking, studying, discovering, and opening to answers. The result has been connection and communication with the unseen...and, of course, *The Witch's Cloak,* which details many essential stepping stones of my journey.

As this memoir approached publication, however, something felt missing. Snippets and story parts pointed to a mysterious gap. Numerous clues left a pale inky trail that teased and taunted, like a jigsaw puzzle haunted by the absence of one wayward piece – a hole trying to overshadow the whole.

One day, as I wandered among the cryptic fragments, the mysterious gap spoke. Whispering in the corners of my mind, it led me to the missing piece, a prologue of sorts – an overview of my existential pursuits, an introduction to the unseen, and a backdrop for my psychic and empathic history. All add shape and context to the chapters that follow.

BROAD STROKES

I look across the valley into a great expanse, witnessing my evolution.

I am, just as you are, a creation of Source.

I am, just as you are, as old as time.

What you see of me now is but an echo of that eternity.

I am light, wrapped in personality and matter, living an earth life for one single purpose: to remember who I am in Truth.

*I am a Child of God
connected with the whole world.*

This is, indeed, the case for us all, ever moving toward that realization, the awareness of who we really are:

Spirit having an Earth adventure.

Sadly, our incarnation (in the flesh) has resulted in much forgetting – forgetting our inheritance and staying blind to our unique spark of divinity.

I know that I was.

For years, murky amnesia seemed to shroud me. As a result, I played in the illusionary fog of material existence, wading through mundane earthy tasks and struggling with life. Overwhelmed and confused, I collected more mistruths and seemed disconnected from my Self. Yes, I was asleep. Asleep, until I began to *awaken* from my fog-filled nightmare.

This is, in truth, the case for humankind. Awaken, we must.

Awakening – a process of coming to understand, know, and express our sacred light – is unique to each person. My awakening began as an ardent, existential quest. I sought answers, always answers.

At first, it was my childhood history that I longed to understand and fully heal. Intimately entwined with this drive was a need to find evidence of and connection to a greater power. Recognizing my deep desire to weave psychology and spirituality – to live in a consciousness where these two worked in unison, supporting and clarifying our earthy and spiritual nature – came only in retrospect.

Everyone seeks answers to life for their own reasons. As I've said, mine was a desire to understand personal events and their connection to something greater. Fueling this, though, was overwhelming anxiety. So, I began to dig. Turning to what I knew (psychology), I took a long reach into general self-development to make sense of myself and my past.

Self-development – the pursuit of getting to know our personality and what makes us tick – is typically relegated to the psychological realm. However, I found that self-development heralds the beginning of a more profound journey, a dive into spirituality. For many that connection may sound curious because our notions about spirituality elicit thoughts of church, creed, or the Bible, leaving self-development solely in the psychological realm. Additional conditioning by religious and cultural mindsets, might cause us to believe that spirituality is entirely separate from us, a place or thing "out-there" that we must discover by searching externally – to a god in the sky, an intermediary in clergy, or in old dictates that keep Source and humans apart.

I, too, had often confused spirituality with religion, confining my connection with Source to words, dogma, and rules of engagement. Thankfully, instead of this archaic, fear-based view and "other-than-me" mindset, I eventually came to learn this...

Religion – humankind's attempt to define the Sacred Forces in and around us – may offer inroads or weave gossamers through our mystical discoveries, but spirituality is so much more. It's highly personal, multidimensional, and uniquely ours. Most importantly, spirituality is not something separate from us but...

- ❀ the essence of who we are – Spirit [4] expressed in form and unconditionally loved by Source;
- ❀ the innate good and virtuous wholeness that lies in our soul and Spirit; and
- ❀ our true Selves as Source knows us to be.

Spirituality looks within – to the sacred flow of Life, to our intimate and integral interconnected beingness, to our holy aspect unified with the world. Through con-

---

[4] The distinction between lower case spirit versus upper case Spirit is meant to signify the energy of those who passed (spirit) as compared to the energy of Source (Spirit).

scious and opening awareness, we can witness and appreciate every plant, insect, animal, and human as joined – *One* through the sacred, unifying thread of Cosmic Essence. Then, and only then, can we experience everything as part of us and we a part of everything.

The Universe is incomplete without each of us, and that includes every living thing.[5]

So, getting to know our earthly life is an integral part of uncovering our spirituality. This journey – the subterranean digging into anything that shrouds our seemingly mysterious and holy core – starts with self-reflection. Here we explore layers of personality patterns, stripping away old beliefs to access our true Self and bask in Its beauty.

Frequently, it's our pain, though, that pulls us to discovery's door, wanting to shed anxiety, sadness, hurts, and negative memories (as I did). But as we do the work required to find relief, we can uncover the deeper aspects of our being. Call it self-development, call it healing, call it spirituality. All roads, eventually, lead us Home.

Now, back to my journey. As you know, I started with a search for clarity, mainly to relieve my discomfort. I didn't have to look far to see the accumulative effects of nuclear family dysfunction and crazy multi-generational dynamics – domestic violence, addiction, incest, rape,

---

[5] Based on the quote, "God Himself is incomplete without me," from ACIM T9:VI-45. Helen Schucman, *A Course in Miracles: Original Edition.*, (Omaha, Nebraska: Course in Miracles Society, 2006).

catastrophic deaths, holocaust trauma, famine, physical abuse, psychological abuse, and emotional neglect and abandonment. It did take me years, though, to remember, collect stories, compare, and recover the hidden parts of myself that family, as well as social conditioning, helped create.

To some onlookers, the panorama of my first 20+ years merely demonstrated a collection of very challenging experiences. However, many scars remained hidden, or so it seemed, under a polished exterior.

Clearly, I didn't choose an easy journey, but I don't bemoan my years here. Instead, I give warm acknowledgment to my personal reality, particularly regarding the past. And while that past is gone (Hallelujah!), it is one that drew me to self-healing, brought me into the world of psycho-spiritual service, is a touchstone for the ways I help others.

I feel truly blessed by the direction in which my unique narrative propelled me – challenging learning opportunities counterbalanced by profound growth. Now, gratitude has replaced old pain. Along with it, recognition of my progress and the wealth of wisdom I cultivated in this short blip called "my life."

> The obstacles in our path are not blocking us – they are redirecting us. Their purpose is not to interfere with our happiness; it is to point us toward new routes to our happiness, new possibilities, new doorways.
>
> ~ Barbara De Angelis

LINES of TIME

In retrospect, the timeline of my journey demonstrates how healing came in stages, levels that took me progressively deeper. Think – uncomfortable peeling and prepping of an onion: tears, skin-staining odor, diced digestible pieces, and more tears until we get to consume the fruits of our labor.

As I stated earlier, I dove into self-development first, and in my mid-20s, the purely psychological understanding of my past began to take shape. A graduate program in group psychotherapy played a significant role. This formal education provided vital information on the significance of our first seven years, though I saw how the first eighteen also hold importance.

Because our early life (in form) deeply impacts and (in)forms the rest, our personal history holds many clues. Mine certainly did. Specifically, I came to understand how messages from primary caretakers, siblings, and friends built a detailed mold for life – a template of attitudes and beliefs about myself, my Self, and the world. Like everyone, I've had to face this internal scaffolding – the good, the bad, and the ugly.

While my "stories" thankfully held critical life lessons – opportunities for transformation – many replayed during adolescence like broken records and seemed compounded by even more subsequent events. All mirrored the adopted viewpoints which shaped my psyche and the not-good-enough attitude that cloaked my light. My mold/belief system was damaged and toxic, misshapen and cracked by trauma and dysfunction. However, exploration and examination brought a growing awareness of my compulsion to repeat the past (repetition compulsion), a common human trend. Finally, I had a way to examine the foundation upon which I build relationships. As such, I came to see the very same mold as one to outgrow, reshaping myself in new and healthier ways.

As a handful of the why's and what's came into sharper focus in my twenty-something self, there was growth. Moving into my 30s, vital spiritual threads decorated the edges of my awareness. During this decade, I explored alternative medicine through herbalism and dove into whole foods. Next, came hungry feeding on New Age material – books on past lives, as well as a scientific and hypnotherapeutic study of reincarnation. I urgently tried to tie this "new" information to the unanswered questions left by psychological texts.

As the need to find answers inadvertently morphed into a quest for truth, plenty of people – professionals, colleagues, friends, and authors – offered their opinions and insights along the way. However, when these voices spoke of fate, destiny, and/or happenstance, a deeper part of me knew there was considerably more. So, I outright refused the mindset that "bad things just happen to good people" and became stubbornly bent on clarity, which resulted in a laser-like focus on two questions:

1) Where was God during all my chaos?

2) Why did He/She/It seem to plop me down in the middle of it? In other words, why did the profoundly painful events of my life happen in the first place, and who was responsible?

I was convinced a "real" why, a "true" why existed for feeling alone, afraid, and in pain – a reason other than the life-just-happens answer. Dead set on finding it, I started to feel like I was getting somewhere. Finally.

Despite this progress, in other ways, palpable fear shrouded the exploration of my 30s. In fact, this fear countered my desire to learn with another pattern that looked like this:

1) Explore a New Age book on psychic skills, tarot, or Wicca. *[Yay!]*

2) Start reading it with fervor. *[Woohoo!]*

3) Get to chapter two. *[Panic.]*

4) Close book while treading an anxiety attack. *[Panting.]*

5) Find a new book and start over. *[Yay!]*

6) Repeat steps 2 – 5 ad nauseum. *[Sigh.]*

One part of me could sense a great precipice of knowledge while another mysteriously cowered in dread from something ancient and deadly: repeating the past-life torture and execution for being a healer, psychic, Druid, and witch. (This I know only in retrospect.) As a result, I never finished a single book on psychic development, Wicca, or similar, trendy New Age topics.

From where I now stand, my attempted deep dive seems so superficial...like wading through the shallows to avoid the great abyss. Thankfully, there was no stopping me. And no matter how slow the process, I determinedly kept marching.

Another hallmark of this decade (late in my 30s) was greater clarity regarding early trauma around abuse and the next step in my journey. One vivid memory stands out.

Turning to a healer who did angel card readings and intuitive work, I had my first conscious encounter with Yeshua (Master Jesus), who visited us in the session and told me "to forgive my parents." (I'll never forget how the healer turned three shades of white.) She also urged me to begin automatic writing in the middle of the night, as Spirit was already waking me for the task.

For years, I bypassed what this healing offered. And even though my reading illuminated help that psychology had barely touched on – forgiveness – it was not the answer I expected. How I wish I had listened sooner, but I just wasn't ready for that kind of remedy. Moreover, my willingness and current capabilities rested elsewhere.

Nevertheless, the turmoil of my 30s continued to press me toward hidden answers. Understanding the repetition compulsion pointed the way, along with exploring the influences of past lives, but the whole picture still wasn't in focus. Investigating what I could between married life, diapers, and part-time counseling work, one year bled into the next until I hit critical mass, otherwise known as an even bigger crisis.

True to form for many, there's nothing like a crisis to lead us to Source. Mine came through a chaotic divorce in my 40s, which propelled me onto a dedicated spiritual path. Recalling that transformative time, I now see it as an unusual amalgam: the painful stripping-away of all that I held dear while being superglued to a bullet train. Truth is, this hot mix of hurt and exhilaration, pain and new possibilities, brought profound metamorphosis – a reconnection with myself (and my Self) through deeper layers of spirituality.

Finally, I began to grasp life and its higher lessons. Moreover, I started to feel alive, instead of just surviving.

METAPHYSICS SNAPSHOT

Before we go any further, we must take a brief but necessary diversion to talk about the unseen and my relationship with it. Suffice it to say, giving labels to the unseen – to what seems beyond labeling – can be challenging, but I shall endeavor to differentiate and explain.

In the past several years, I've come to see myself and the world as Divine Design in expression. The shift arrived first as a mental construct and eventually grew into a heartfelt knowing. Source (Divine Design) is an energy, and all energy, in truth, is of Source – the Intelligence that creates and ever becomes more through vibrations of love and benevolence.

Source is an intimate part of all life, an energy that is everywhere and *connects* all things. Like luminous strands of light that reach out into the whole, the "web" of Sacred Flow touches into all, unifying the seen and unseen, well beyond our five senses.

Through our connection with Divine energy, each of us can create like Source and communicate with Her/Him/ It in our own unique way. The means for that communication is our intuition, the voice of the Divine within us.

Intuition often registers as a feeling, a knowing beyond logic or fact, frequently sensed within our core. The reason is this: a nerve bundle called the solar plexus – a physical manifestation behind the stomach, fed by the third chakra,[6] and linked to our Feeling Nature.[7] Think gut feeling, sixth sense, vibes…

Believe it or not, you and all of life have a direct line to Source – animals and plants via instinct and humans through intuition (as well as through love, joy, peace, ideas, inspiration, etc.). Intuition is a conduit of higher understanding, guidance, direction, etc. that comes to you by working *through* you – the energetic vibration through which each person uniquely attunes to Intelligent Force.

If intuition is Source speaking through us, what about psychic abilities? Many people believe that being psychic – the "talent" of reading detailed unseen information about others, events, situations, etc. – is a gift to only some. And by in large, the world believes that only recognized psychics can speak to what lies beyond our five senses.

To complicate matters, associations with the term psychic can be somewhat mixed between the mysterious, frightening, and even ominous. So, let me set the record straight…

We are all psychic.

Yes. You, me, Aunt Jane, the garbage man. The difference is that some of us have spent lifetimes honing the skill and can employ it with greater clarity or accuracy. So can you, with practice.

---

[6] See *Glossary*.
[7] See *Glossary*.

To act psychically is to *sense and respond* to information expressed as energy. This happens through the clairs – clairvoyant (clear vision), clairaudient (clear sound), claircognizant (clear thought/knowing/telepathy) and clairsentient (clear feeling). Psychics read what others hold in their energy field or aura,[8] namely pain, beliefs, soul memory, physical health, and current attitudes/ moods.

Because everything is energy, we can glean psychic information from literally anything: plants, animals, places,[9] Mother Earth, and people. We can even read objects (psychometry), getting data on their creators and owners, which unravels the object's history, much like reading people does.

How might you, personally, be psychic? Well, you'll have to answer the finer detail of that yourself, but here's a typical example that demonstrates everyone's general psychic attunement:

Let's say you walked into a party. Suddenly, you spot a person across the room, someone you've never met. Suppose, without any logical reason, you're immediately aware that you don't like the person. You don't know why or how, but you can just feel a sense of dislike. You may even find yourself retracting from them, moving phys- ically away, or feeling the need to keep your distance. Simultaneously, beyond your conscious knowing, your aura responds to your aversion by pulling closer to your

---

[8] Everything, inanimate or animate, has an energy field – a field of elec- tromagnetic energy known as an aura.

[9] The energy of places is a combination of the area's mass conscious- ness, the land, and collective history.

physical form, away from the person.[10] The sudden dislike, feeling of retraction, and pulling back of your aura
are all a result of your psychic nature – the innate and
subconscious reading of and responding to another's
energy. This example communicates a vibrational "mis-
match" between you and another and an attunement that
results in unconscious energetic protection. And while
the opposite may occur, feeling drawn to another, we still
behave consistently, naturally, and automatically psychic.

This begs another question: How do psychic faculties
differ from mediumship? While the world (and many
mediums) like to differentiate between psychic and
mediumistic abilities, the skillset falls on a continuum of
developing awareness and attunement. Mediums have
practiced (again from other lifetimes) the ability to read
auras, as well as communicate with a range of entities
that can include disincarnate spirits, angels, guides, spirit
teachers, and/or their Higher Self. It's something anyone
can practice by matching the vibration of their desired
connection.

Mediumship operates much like musical resonance:

Among the amazing properties of sound is
resonance, which occurs when one object pulsating
at a natural frequency compels a second object into
vibrational motion. We can understand resonance
most easily through musical instruments. Let's
imagine for a moment two violins side by side.
Pluck the D string on just one violin, and the D
string on the other vibrates in unison at the very

[10] Rev. Penny Donovan, *Consciously Planning Your Life* (video), (Albany, NY: Sacred Garden Fellowship, 1995).

same pitch. This occurs with no contact to the accompanying violin. The frequency of vibration of one instrument calls forth the same vibration of its partner – musical resonance in action."[11]

Instead of sound and notes, we must make our connection across the veil through the frequency of unconditional love – the universal language of higher beings – and the energies held by a specific entity. Raising our vibration up and out of the heavy earth plane facilitates this communication. So, the higher the energy of the being, the higher we must go to meet their vibration. From lowest to highest (generally speaking) are passed-over loved ones and disincarnate spirits, then guides, teachers, angels, and finally our Higher Self. If, for example, we want to communicate with the finer vibrations of angels or our Higher Self, we must continue to rise in our consciousness beyond any personality limitations that contaminate the information.

This brings us, next, to empathic or energy-sensitive constitutions. We all can possess empathy, the capacity to step into another person's shoes and understand their situation, struggles, feelings, etc. (Notice, I said "can," as some people incarnate or become devoid of this capacity in alignment with their current personality.) An empathic constitution, however, is like empathy on steroids. Specifically, empaths regularly absorb vibrations nearby and from others, wearing them like invisible borrowed clothes. In other words, people's moods, attitudes, illnesses, and unhealed aspects can be the dirty psychic

[11]Adriene Nicastro, *The Soul-Discovery Journalbook: An Intimate Journey into Self, Volume III,* (Bellefonte, PA: Pathways to Freedom Press, 2021), p. 239.

laundry unconsciously worn by these sensitive creatures. Furthermore, the more negative energy an empath personally holds/experiences, the more prone they become to carry another's challenging energetic state. Think, Velcro ball in a dryer full of lint. Yes, yuck! (Trust me, I know!) And while empathic qualities manifest uniquely to the person, many similarities among energy-sensitives exist, falling on a continuum of intensity. (See *An Empath's Checklist.*)

ON BEING EMPATHIC

While I've been empathic my whole life, I only began to understand it in the last twelve years. Instead, I spent decades as a nervous tuning fork – consumed with worry, vibrating at the level of those around me, and piloting days through all I absorbed from my surroundings, unaware of what was mine.

During my first astrological reading with a fellow spiritual student, I learned the term "psychic sponge" (someone who absorbs dirty energy like a nondiscrimin-atingly porous kitchen scrubber). Yep, that was me, taking on others' internal climate and making it my own storm. Until then, I had resigned myself to the idea that I was strange, perhaps even crazy, and that life was weird and too complicated.

I've always been a sensitive creature; so sensitive, though, that I've been in more trouble for it than not. It made my mother highly irritated and brought out her punitive side, a nightmare for an empathic child. But, outside that environment wasn't always better. Some hated that I could read people or situations; others criticized my intuitive assessments, labeling me as judgmental or too imaginative, only to later return abashed and confirming my assessments.

Don't get me wrong: feeling repeatedly criticized, dismissed, questioned, and/or judged can be tough. So, on the one hand, these experiences produced unwanted results as incessant self-doubt (a lifelong lesson for me). But, there also was a fantastic upside: an opportunity to transform the root cause of my insecurity through blooming and fortification of trust – in myself, in my ability to understand situations/people, in my intuition, and in Source. Not a bad bargain, just a long process in the making.[12]

Other curious empathic experiences included (and still do) a need to be cautious about all forms of media – music, books, videos, movies, TV, and photographs. For example, while my high-school classmates hungrily consumed horror flicks with Freddie Kruger, I still clung to *Little House on the Prairie*.

Perhaps you think that I was sheltered. Not the case, at least not with that. I just felt too overwhelmed by anything bloody, violent, or frightening. However, when morbid curiosity or peer pressure won out, my consumption would make me physically sick. This happened the

---

[12] The Spiritual Law of Cause and Effect operates unerringly on multiple levels, a full range of energies from the playing out of karma to the expression of unity. You can witness The Law of Cause and Effect in my life in this way: it's because I questioned myself (cause) that I manifested so many situations that made me question myself (effect). The reason: a lack of belief in Self and self, unfolding in my environment as experiences in which I felt doubted and/or lacked trust in myself or others. In alignment with other ancient spiritual principles, the Law of Cause and Effect is an out-picturing of the Hermetic teaching, "as within, so without"; this means that life is *always* a projection of our internal climate. In other words, what we believe reveals itself in our life as situations that demonstrate those beliefs.

night I watched one horrifying scene from *Lord of the Flies*, causing me to nearly puke and spend the following days nauseated.

Simply said, I've seriously paid for watching emotionally stimulating, graphic, or violent content. As such, it has repeatedly resulted in unintentional, extended viewing – scenes stuck on rewind/replay as a neural racetrack of images loop for days. Frequently, whatever I consumed was also enough to significantly contaminate my dreams, making restful sleep impossible.

Music is another medium that requires mindfulness. While slightly less annoying, a musical merry-go-round, like my problems with overwhelming movies, can disturb my peace. This is especially true with songs that I love. The more intense my emotional response, the greater chance a catchy tune will land on automatic play and drive me utterly bonkers, like a record needle stuck in a scratch. Don't get me wrong: I love music and even grew up playing multiple instruments. And while I listen to many genres when the mood strikes, you'll find our home quiet most days, except for songbirds, rain, and wind. So, yes, I adore silence. (I'd like to meet an empath that doesn't.)

You may be wondering how media can affect someone so much. The reason is this: psychic junk stuck in our aura like energetic chiggers that stimulate repetitive thoughts, images, or sounds. Think, mental carousel...uncannily like OCD. The more potent the auric attachment, the more like energy[13] it collects, growing in intensity and drawing our attention. In other words, the "junk" (thoughts

---

[13] **Like energy** – vibrations of a similar frequency attracted to one another; similar emotions, feelings, and thoughts that magnetically collect.

magnetized by feelings as a form sitting in our aura) builds through repetitive focus. This happens to everyone, but empaths are more intensely affected by or aware of the energetic presence.

Thankfully, I have tools now, but in my mid-30s, I intuitively and energetically reached a natural saturation point with media. This occurred first with the news when, one day, I just abruptly stopped watching it. My decision for this permanent fast fell on the heels of three tear-filled nights, witnessing the devastating 2004 tsunami in India. (You may remember it as the deadliest tsunami in recorded history. Utter ruin.) Long before I fully understood the culminating effect of negative media, ending its onslaught became one of the best decisions I ever made. No regrets, not one. That's not to say that I don't care about what happens to others or feel for their plight. I simply know that my pain or overload won't help those beleaguered by the same. And while my knowledge about events might lag compared to the average media consumer, the payoff has been staggeringly positive. Media abstention helps keep my consciousness in a space to offer love, light, and healing to a world in much need.

Next in the empath's playbook, we come to the years of wearing nothing but black, white, or some comfortable combination of the two. The particular crowd, the emotional atmosphere, and my role in any situation always influenced this monotone dress code. Comments like, "I never see you in anything colorful" became routine, but did not deter me. Little did I know, I unintentionally cloaked my energy; it just felt right. Wrapping myself in the element of night or buffering through the crystal-whiteness of clouds was just one way I could avoid feeling vulnerable, like a deer walking across an open field in hunting season. Black (cloaking) and white (protective) was an energetic decision that I honored but didn't understand until my 40s.

In addition to these quirky but typical empathic sensitivities, there was also a broad range of negative side effects in the feels department. Many times, anger, anxiety, and sometimes guilt culminated in a rollercoaster of emotions – attitudes projected from others. These I carried without realizing it. For example, when my children cried (especially as babies), their distress registered as extreme discomfort in me; I could never let them cry it out in the crib. Ever. Even their pain or illness would register as the same pain or symptoms in my body. If there was even the threat of pain, like an avoided bicycle crash or a near-skinned knee, a jolt of electricity would hit my solar plexus like a finely tuned alarm.

Another example, a more extreme and disturbing experience, happened when I carried suicidal impulses from a college roommate still healing from a recent suicide attempt. Years later, I connected the dots, realizing the odd and arbitrary urges (minus any depression, anxiety, or any related personal symptoms) to jump through my dorm window belonged to someone else – a sweet soul struggling with emotional pain and torment.

Until I learned to manage energy, life was quite a carnival ride. Gathering vibrations like a collection of wayward pets, I brought energy from one situation or person to another. Additionally, the blurred lines and boundaries between myself and others made personal experiences seem compounded with every interaction. As such, energetic sensitivity chronically amplified my relationships (the casual and the more intimate ones) as my feelings intensified with what others carried and/or projected on me. Let me offer an example.

Imagine a quarrel, one between a friend and me, someone we'll call Red. In this situation, I would grapple with quite the collection – a blend of my feelings about Red from past interactions, the thoughts/emotions about our disagreement, Red's feelings/thoughts about me, and any hurt or upset experienced by Red in the conflict – and carry ALL of it. Think…toxic milkshake.

But the problem wasn't just with friends like Red. Significant internal turmoil became a constant companion, a yuck-bag of worms that I dragged with me as the tangled emotions, thoughts, and attitudes I couldn't separate from my own. To complicate matters, manipulative and/or defensive folks, the ones who refused to take responsibility for their behaviors or reactions, added more layers to the dynamics. In truth, I can't point to being empathic as the only cause. Conditioning based on family entanglement and unhealthy interactions played a large part, past programming that blended profoundly with my psychic-sponge constitution. So, anyone and everyone's yuck, that I was trained to carry, just felt like mine.

To gain clarity, I needed to reconcile several layers: my reaction to what transpired, the other person's reaction, and the strange amalgam of all the energies between us. Eventually, I learned to separate my thoughts/emotions from the mix, deal with the entangled/destructive family patterns, and protect my energy. Yes, I learned to stand in my power.

It's fair to say my work in this arena has been years in the making.

PSYCHIC FLOWERS

Long before I knew what I saw, heard, or sensed, the energy of spirit hung around me in the ethers, like a sleepy mist awaiting discovery. Blame it on my empathic constitution or Hollywood, but the spirit world, in many ways, seemed to generate more fear than reassurance. When I was a child, my chaotic household complicated this feeling of uneasiness. (Truly, it wouldn't take much contemplation to make a list of events and people that contributed to my constant internal climate – nervous anticipation, vigilance, and knowing-but-not-knowing.)

Still, an overarching sense of the unseen remained palpable but amorphous for many years. At first, it manifested as a tangible fear of the dark, keeping me in well-lit rooms even during sleep. This lasted into grade school. But even now, when the unseen holds a certain thickness (frequently from those passed-over), the hair on my neck stands erect and a feeling of eeriness permeates my nervous bones. This, despite all I've learned.

While a particular uneasiness around the unseen wove its way through childhood, so did the desire to know more. Early memories of practicing psychic faculties include something I later called the psychic game – one that I created to play with Nana (my grandmother-like nanny). On days that I couldn't be outside, I would drag her away from afternoon soaps to join me on the large area rug in the living room. While she hid objects unknown to me under a pillow, I would "guess" one by one at what she selected from the pile of goodies. Nana always made me feel that I had "the gift" with expressions of congratulatory surprise for correct predictions. To this day, I don't know if she was merely placating me or amazed at my accuracy. Interestingly, the game continued into adolescence with my mother, one she was happy to indulge.

Through the years, tapping further into the spirit world happened unconsciously. Flashes of shadows, shapes, or even detailed figures frequently appeared in my peripheral vision. (Something common for those attuned to the unseen.) More times than I can count, I would simultaneously feel a presence but be fooled, time and again, into thinking something physical stood out of my direct vision. As I turned toward the very "thing" that drew me, my questioning eyes would stare straight into nothingness – no figure or shape – just air with an odd, opaque lingering. Years later, the psychic signature of visiting spirit is no longer a mystery.

Objective witnessing – where spirit appeared directly in front of me – came rarely and only through spirit animals. The first of such events arrived one twilight evening, while the very last sliver of sun dipped below the horizon. As my mom, Ammy (my grandmother), and my wispy three-year-old self approached the kitchen door, I felt "pulled" to the shaded space between our garage and another outbuilding. There, my curiosity was met by an impressively bushy-maned lion with a beautiful golden coat. His piercing coal-like eyes silently stared back with patience, noble resolve, and velvety power. Fear would have been a proportionate response toward such a sight, especially as a tiny child; however, I wasn't afraid. Filled with surprise and awe, I wanted to share my new friend with mom, but this only brought her disbelief and disdain. Shaming for a "made up a story like that" left a lingering wound that perpetuated self-doubt.

Though I was a mere toddler, the memory of my lion's kingly appearance remains tattooed on my soul, the mystical alchemy of gilded detail, majestic presence, and total protection. Disregard for speaking truth has become replaced with praise for that inner child, helping her believe in her innate power and abilities. Interestingly, lions became a harbinger of my path and the promise of Animal Medicine in years to come.

African Male Lion

Wisdom as an ancient sage; assertion as feminine power: connection to the sun and thus God; counsel for courage and strength; safety regardless of appearances, benevolent leadership, inner fortitude by mastering emotions; lessons with groups and community: patient and affectionate motherhood; and cultivating centeredness in our core power.[14]

MY NEW FAMILY

It's fair to say that connection with spirit had been a life-long desire but not consistently acted upon until I found a spiritual community called Sacred Garden Fellowship (SGF).[15] Studying with the teachers of SGF offered the means to consciously open my talents for mental mediumship – visions, impressions, smells, sounds, and thoughts in my mind's eye through the sixth chakra or third eye chakra. And while I've spent years of focused study to develop this ability to be a conduit of healing for

---

[14] Presley Love, Lion Symbolism & Lion Meaning / 9 *Spiritual Meanings of the Lion*, n.d., universeofsymbolism.com. and Ted Andrews, *Animal-Speaks: The Spiritual and Mystical Powers of Creatures Great and Small*, St. Paul, MN: (Llewellyn Productions, 1995).

[15] See Resources.

myself and others, I know, without a doubt, that it's been lifetimes in the making.

Starting in 2008, I began actively studying and practicing psychic work, as well as attending SGF retreats, which continued until 2020. These sacred weekend events generally occurred once per month, a welcome time away from earthly concerns. They were rich with channeled lessons from Master Teachers, self-reflection and insights, spiritual energy healing, and support.

It is, in fact, the past twelve years combined with all that transpired in my life, primarily spiritual evolution, that brought *The Witch's Cloak* into being. For that I am eternally grateful, especially to SGF, my teachers, the channeled entities that guided us all, and the friends I met along the way. For a time, I found the home I needed, a place to grow, and people who accepted me and validated my experiences. At SGF, weird, mystical, metaphysical, and spiritual events were the norm.

GROWTH AND BLOOMING

One distinct upside counterbalances this crazy life, at least for me: many ups and downs generated a deep desire to change my world and help others. As a result, I learned to heal the pain of old trauma, release toxic conditioning, manage emotional reactions to others/situations, and not take on people's moods/energy. And despite any perceived stressors, difficulties, vulner-abilities, or sensitivities, I'm far from a fragile, recoiling woman. Fierceness, strength, determination, resilience, and loyalty stand firmly above any struggles with empathic stress, psychic contamination, worry, trauma, or self-sabotage. Why? Because long ago, I decided that the challenges of this great adventure wouldn't define me. Instead, I chose to use them as a powerful impetus for change and growth. In other words...

the many years of trauma and turmoil became the rocky trail on which I used my spiritual staff for strength, stability, and navigation.

Deep psycho-spiritual work has given me a grace-filled blend of inner peace, humble accomplishment, and genuine gratitude, beautifully painting a different inner landscape. That said, I continue the daily practice of breaking old residual patterns, releasing what doesn't serve my highest good, being a light, holding my center, and staying consciously connected to Source. Yes, life never carries me so far that I forget my journey of awakening. And some days, I still tell myself, *Adriene, you're a work in progress* – a gentle reminder that I am, indeed, human.

Two beautiful children, many loving friendships, a gratifying, intuitively-fueled, private healing practice, as well as my relationship with Source provide the love, joy, and peace that sustain me. In fact, Source is all of it, many threads of light that weave their way into my life, the vital connections across my years, colorful flowers bordering a winding path that offer grace, hope, and the energy to move forward in faith.

Without the Cosmic energy of the unseen, the varied experiences with it and all it has provided, this book wouldn't exist. So, in great gratitude and without further ado, I offer you...

The Witch's Cloak: A Memoir of the Unseen.

The

Witch's

Cloak

A Memoir of the Unseen

In the universe,
there are things that are known,
and things that are unknown,
and in between, there are doors.
~ William Blake

The Witch's Cloak

Inspiration is some mysterious blessing which happens when the wheels are turning smoothly.

- Quentin Blake

We become inspired throughout our lives in many, many ways. Even when we don't recognize the influence of inspiration or if it slips through our consciousness as ordinary thought or feeling, Spirit remains ever present, offering, filling, and moving us. Feelings of warmth and awe that draw us to a summer sunset, the artful creations of food stirred with love, a joy-filled quest for just the right gift, these are Spirit whisperings.

For me, personal inspiration comes mostly through creative outlets. Music, crafts, art, and writing are the very fabric of my DNA, woven through my being like luminous golden threads. They lovingly wrap me in times of turmoil, insistently prod me into action, and give voice to challenging thoughts and feelings that seek resolution.

Creativity has long been my closest and most loyal companion. Look at baby photos and you'll find a paintbrush strangled in my chubby, formula-crusted hand. (Actually, that's an unfulfilled wish. Paint was far too messy for my mom. Pencils and oil pastels were more her speed.) As a small child, I frequently retreated into an inner world, a world birthed into the physical through multi-colored renderings of nature. Escaping outside to wash away the effects of our chaos-filled home, I'd build leaf dwellings for ants, dress up pets, chase field mice, and collect flowers. Wildlife's gifts kept me occupied and nurtured for hours. Still, years later, many forms of nature-inspired arts and crafts are the imaginative endeavors that bring joy, ways to touch into something innate and sacred.

Through all my years of experience, I have witnessed how inspirations surfaced with varying levels of persuasion. They pulled me in fluctuating potencies, calling out for conception, gestation, and birth. Seeds with a voice. Some screamed, others whispered, but none escaped my attention. As a result, I innately cycle through phases and different creative mediums like breathing – a natural and essential rhythm for living.

Do I ever find myself lacking in ideas and inspirations? That would be impossible. Scrapbooking, photography, sketching, sewing, painting, gardening, decorating, writing, or some other activity may poke at my consciousness, each taking turns to make their way into the world. It's fair to say that most days, I feel drawn to a project, drawn like a moth to a flame. The loving energy tugs at my center and ignites a well-spring of passion which flows from my divine internal essence, the same Sacred River that influences us all.

As swirling pools of jubilant anticipation – the check-the-mailbox-for-surprise-deliveries kind of excitement – spark joy and an expression of something much deeper than my little self, frequently, I don't know what will emerge. This is the nature of the witch's cloak...

I want a cloak. The yearning burns in my heart, seemingly out of nowhere.

Accompanied by an image, the idea first appeared in my mind's eye infused with a feeling that pulled me to it, plopping itself down in an I'm-not-moving-until-you-find-this manner. My vision is crystal clear – a long, flowing garment of rich heather-gray wool, fastened at the neck and adorned with a generous hood. The elegant fabric pours over my form, reaching just above the ankle to fall in ample, smoky folds. Its beauty elicits a sense of sophisticated comfort, like being home lounging in my favorite sweatshirt or pajamas...fancy ones, that is.

I'm finding one to buy, is the unwavering determination behind this mysterious push. My mind is made up. Just like that.

Three weeks now, scouring stores and surfing the internet, but nothing to my liking has appeared. Yet, this gray phantom continues to haunt me, sending thoughts to intrude on every part of my day.

I guess I need to make one myself. A not-so-idle intention finds resolution. With it, I take the seed of my cloak's conception on a short journey – the garden of my mind – fertilizing the thought while planting it in the rich soil of my love to coax its growth.

Usually, when an idea presses on me, the urge to move –
to act upon it and help it progress toward completion – is
quite powerful. I feel consumed, again, on fire with creative juice. Hot Southern whiskey that burns, warming my
insides. Intoxicated with enthusiasm, I'm tipsy, yet…
focused.

So, the quest switches gears from a hunt to an altogether
different adventure, and my plan takes form. *A trip to the
fabric store is what I need to do!* As the next logical step
for a seamstress on a mission, I feel certain that I'll get
what I need there.

I'm in heaven, otherwise known as Joanne Fabrics. [*Sigh.*]
Fabric stores are a playground of possibilities. Like craft
or art stores, fabric stores can keep me occupied for hours,
fantasizing and planning my next creation…and the next…
and the next…. (It's easy for me to get carried away, as you
can see.) In truth, stepping into any store that sparks
creativity like Joanne's brings out my tow-headed, waif-
like four-year-old. She skips spiritedly among the racks,
basking in multicolored miracles, seeing something the
adult in me cannot.

We could not be surrounded by more deliciousness. Every
scrap, button, and lace beg to be touched with hands and
eyes, eyes and hands. Intoxication bubbles forth again, and
the four-year-old grins while my grown-up self burps with
Joanne drunkenness.

Weaving in and out of the aisles at a steady pace, my
search feels well underway. Drooling, I peruse bolts and
bolts of every hue and texture. They stand erect and
perfectly aligned, showing off a deserved vanity like tall

cloth storybooks in orderly displays. My eyes flirt with plaids and stripes, called in every direction. Cheeks playfully blush at polka dots and paisleys. *So many to choose from...*

Pay attention! Compare! A chastising thought snaps me back to the mission: to align this myriad of choices with my vision. And so, cloth by cloth, I continue, a gold miner looking for one perfect and gorgeous nugget.

Suddenly, *Eureka!* The perfect gray flannel wool nearly jumps off the rack. The flecks of charcoal and smoky-white sit perfectly balanced with rich slate overtones. Running my fingertips along the delicately woven threads, the four-year-old pipes up in exuberance. *This is it!*

Twenty-nine dollars a yard! A loud hiss escapes my lips as inner-child fantasies meet the reality of capitalism, a reality that undermines a budget begging to be ignored.

Maybe I need to check out patterns first, and then I'll worry about cost.

This internal chatter smooths my inner child's disappointment, and I pause to consider what's next.

Standing motionless under the glaring store lights, *I really hope...no pray...that I don't need yards and yards to do "flowing."*

Damn those visions. They're so demanding!

Marching straight to the back of the store on an unanticipated side route, I feverishly search the pattern section, scrutinizing (the theme for today's adventure) every book available. But tearing through the pages of McCall's, Vogue, Simplicity, and other lesser-known companies, irritation quickly replaces my enthusiasm. Not a single pattern meets the job description. Funny (and not in a humorous way) how convinced I was that my perfect, hooded cloak lay coyly waiting among these carefully engineered designs.

Ugh! Now what? I deliberate, my nimble fingers tapping pensively on piles of books. (I'm not so easily deterred, you know.)

I can do this! My inner coach adds with self-assurance.

Yep, I'm gonna wing it!

So, back to the drawing board. And improvising...

Grabbing a hooded poncho pattern from a nearby open rack, the decision to blend this with others at home now replaces my old plans. A Frankenstein design of sorts – an arm from here and a head from there – mentally merges: begged and borrowed parts to create a whole.

Now to reconnect with my beloved gray wool.

Zigzagging through thread, batting, and zippers, I hum my way back to the fabric section. That's when I see it. Somewhere between the racks of colorful spools and piles of discarded cloth sits a plush-gray, brushed-cotton blend with pale, steely-lavender iridescence. And it serendipitously lies...*DA-DA-DA-DAAAHHHHH*...on the sale table! The unusual texture, I guess, caught my eye, or the angels were jumping up and down on it, waving "HERE!" signs. It's nothing short of a miracle, really, barely visible between all the sloppily stacked layers of miscellaneous material. Barely, that is, except for the magical effects of the overhead fluorescent lights. Coincidently (or not), at four dollars a yard, it is perfect for my squeaky-tight budget!

It's been days since my Joanne's adventure. The material and patterns anxiously wait, sitting in my lair (otherwise known as the studio).

Unlike the supplies, visions poke and prod, urging me to continue my mission. Each insistent flash highlights the cloak's mysterious, graceful length and cavernous hood – a hood spacious enough to conceal the wearer's face. These images guide all ongoing crafting as they flow forth from the fountain of my artistic juices, inspiration in action. At times they seem to occupy their own hazy form, lingering in doorways and over my shoulder, a taskmaster filled with feverish passion.

Steady gestational vibrations stretch and poke the walls of my fertile womb; a developing seed desires birthing. It is, without a doubt, relentless. So, in the moments between working and being a single mom, I cut and patch, figure and place, piecing together one pattern with another as the powerful and seductive energy pulls at me. The synthesis of my curious creation gradually crystallizes into form: a grand amalgamation of poncho, coat, and cape with arms and a fleece lining for warmth and functionality.

Urged to a finale, I work diligently to finish by an upcoming spiritual retreat. Instead, life happens, making my steely-gray handiwork incomplete when its due date arrives. And though this late pregnancy lingers, I pray the extra time will clarify my burning desire to forge ahead.

❖

I'm off to another retreat, the very retreat where I hoped to display weeks-worth of work. Instead, I arrive empty-handed, but I'm not disappointed. Our sacred weekends are potent, and I'm ready for whatever Spirit delivers.

These retreats offer the space and opportunity to offer many spiritual energy healings – the transmission of energy through the healer, followed by intuitive, psychic, or mediumistic messages to help complete the process. Using intuition and psychic faculties, I find the room to practice and grow through the weekend with all it holds. And so, I employ my gifts in ongoing evolution.

Up until now, most psychic information has come to me as feelings – clairsentience, to be precise. Sometimes I see images or visions aligned with mental mediumship, but they are currently brief and wispy.

It doesn't take long for me to discover that change is afoot. The energy flows now with ease. With it a new faculty emerges from the unseen, like the Universe flipped a switch, a mental video player projecting in my sixth chakra. Colorful 3D graphics in long-running scenes unfold in my mind's eye during each healing. What I share with the group meets with confirmation from other participants, those I trust much more than myself.

Another "side-effect" comes to light. Buzzed and excited with my "new ability" – tapping into the Akashic Records to witness past lives of those receiving healing – creates an unusual but welcome exuberance. It's considerably more than I anticipated.

❖

The weekend progresses, learning and doing healings. Then on Saturday afternoon, the group readies to send healing to Marie, a member unable to attend until later this evening. We all envision her with us in our hearts and minds to offer remote healing. As such, the group lovingly connects to one another and Marie, heart to heart and Spirit to Spirit. For me, a doorway opens and once again, vivid images flood my mind's eye...

Deep in the woods, freshly fallen snow sits silently, a blanket of blanched, iridescent crystals that cover everything around me. It contrasts the sleepy, gray-brown branches.

I see Marie. She is walking with me on a wide path between the naked trees. We chat and giggle as our feet make first tracks across the untouched whiteness. Something else curiously drops into my awareness – matching long, gray, hooded wool cloaks. (You might think at this point that I'd be jumping out of my chair, screeching, "There it is! There it is!" However, this isn't the nature of Spirit or this kind of work. In truth, the information and energy drift in softly, as a quiet knowing. So, instead, I feel more of an "of course.")

As I continue to observe, the most brutal pieces of this vision remain hidden, resting on the cutting room floor. It's better this way, concealed. Regardless, the conclusion is clear: this lifetime, like many others connected with the healing arts, took a tragic turn. I know this from the brightly divergent crimson hues of life essence that tarnish the pure white landscape. It's all the evidence required to signal our unwelcome ending.

I focus on the stained snow, hoping for a different conclusion. But what bubbles forth without warning is a vicious sense of wrong-doing, malignantly laced with its twin – guilt. My gut sits disquieted, tinged with a whisper of something else: the question of why, why this guilt? The answer is offered before the thought is even complete. I either brought her into the craft or the woods that day, and I'm not sure which. Whatever the case, it appears to have sealed our fate and created self-blame.

In our barren resting place, Marie and I joined the many, many thousands of other healers, midwives, seers, and herbalists known to the masses as witches. Other than my vision, no signposts or words inform me of this; it's just a feeling that settles like an icy chill into my very bones.

When Marie finally arrives to join the group, I share the vision...the snow, the cloak, and the death we healed, together. It's a story she already knows, having received the lifetime during a reading in Lily Dale, a lifetime from Salem during the witch trials.

Taking in the news and confirmation from Marie, I try to absorb all that transpired. Multiple feelings flood in and compete for residence, but one thing stands steadfast in my heart: I know the origin of my gray cloak.

Why did this memory press so powerfully on my consciousness? Why now? Because my soul, moving with definite purpose, brought the gray wrapping as a delivery from the unseen. While it was meant to soothe and calm, the cloak, first, became a necessary catalyst for healing, a way to prepare me for deeper transformation. And as its memory's hideout turned thin and vaporous by weeks of unconscious preparation, what surfaced finally opened the way for vital work – to reconcile a lifetime that ended early, abruptly, and with physical, mental, and emotional suffering.

Like all healing through the cleansing energy of Source, I was able to surrender what no longer served me, unblocking my way for another journey, restored and ready to assist others do the same. This is the nature of spiritual work – everything in life offering clues, lessons, and opportunities for awakening.

I feel thankful that the cloak was a harbinger of sacred weaving, an appeal from Spirit to release my fear as a budding lightworker and to courageously walk the path before me. So, I must trust my past to remain in the past. History will not repeat itself. No fear, no guilt, only forgiveness.

I'm back in my studio, resting in completion. Spellbinding and cosmic gardening – a seed planted in the rich humerus of my mind, sewn with the threads of desire, and watered with love – has made me full. She is a beauty. On cold winter days, she reminds me of healing, profound change, and a powerful legacy that's woven into her very substance.

Now, the cloak sparks a different vision, one born of new healing...

The wood crackles, a pile of burning branches consumed in a central light. Tendrils of fire lick the air, dragon's tongues that radiate out into the darkness, heating the space around us.

The summer grass tickles my bare feet, pressing on the edges and between toes like papery feathers in mottled green hues. Hands join in the warmth of the fire, a circle of women connected in Sisterhood, cemented by love. We are the siblings of nature, of helping and healing, bound to one another through a common desire. There is overwhelming adoration of the Blessed One within, the One Who binds all, like threads of a sacred cloth woven in eternal harmony.

As sparks escape the fire, rising into the inky-black sky and traveling to the heavens, we cast our shadows on Mother Earth and one another. All are affected, joined heart to heart, soul to soul, and Spirit to Spirit.

Union is the namesake of our vigil. Our light – inner and outer – reaches across the field, across the night sky, across time to mark the New. We are the birthing and nurturing of all that's pure and heart-centered.

Standing together, like a steely needle piercing the fabric of time, we stretch and pull, bringing the Universe to a single point, a grand peaked tent of past and present unconfined by conventional clocks ticking.

As the New miraculously expands into the Infinite, we swell with It, until time outside of time is all that remains. No pain. No suffering. No separation. Only Eternity and our place in It.

I witness our weaving – intimacy with the New, our shining, our Sisterhood – and I am healed.

❖

Reflections

❖ *Do you have inspirations and ideas that stand out in your mind?*

❖ *Can you see them as valuable gifts?*

❖ *Did your inspirations or ideas rest on the wings of a lesson?*

❖ *How did what you learned change your life?*

❖ *Can you recognize the significance of these gifts and opportunities?*

Cosmic Melodies

Music is moonlight in the gloomy night of life.
- Jean Paul

Our consciousness, an evolving aspect of our being, expands or contracts through our experiences. This internal movement can grow in openness or close through fear, depending on our beliefs and how they influence our responses to life. Because we commonly gravitate to what we know, resting in how we have made sense of the world, our feelings of safety and comfort erect parameters and certain bookends. But giving ourselves the freedom – to think, express, and stretch outside our own back yard, beyond our comfort zone – to challenge our perceived limits, can lead us in the most unexpected ways. We might adopt different world views, broaden our horizons, or discover a whole new vivacity.

Perhaps our exploration will even draw us to the unseen – spirituality, the metaphysical, and conscious higher guidance through our intuition. This kind of journey can take us to the depth of our soul to uncover a beautiful inner landscape where mystical treasures await. It can also lead us into great adventures if we allow ourselves to trust, staying open to all that might unfold.

Humankind, as a collective, has opened in consciousness, the New Age movement a signpost. Somewhat less so in the past ten to twenty years but still present, however, is the tendency for "truth" to remain confined by what's tangible, proven through physical measurements and scientific analyses. As such, the world still meets mystical or psychic experiences with skepticism, generating feelings that range from awe and curiosity to shock and worry. And if you align most with mindsets that support logic, linear thinking, or proof, fear of trickery or subterfuge may mar your experiences.

On a deeper level, the more meaningful and profound any event, the more risk it will challenge all we've learned. That said, when we limit truth to what's measurable, tangible, or verified by others through the five senses, a whole world becomes lost to us, and certain doors to the Universe remain closed.

I, too, despite all my unusual and spiritual experiences, can still question my psychic impressions and intuition. Sometimes old programming – the tapes that say, "It's just imagination if you don't have solid evidence" – can be hard to ignore. But at other times, the unseen surfaces with such potency that it grabs my attention and refuses to let go. That's just what happened...

It's January. The wind whistles sharply, and newly fallen snow blankets the landscape under a star-filled, blue-black night. The sun has long been gone, but I stay awake to read as the clock ticks toward midnight. My two little ones sleep soundly across the quiet hallway.

Nestling beneath mounds of heavy covers, the evening plodding along peacefully, I engross myself in spiritual material. Except for the icy cold gusts intermittently ruffling the vinyl siding, there's a hush that compounds the stillness inside. Only the haunting echos of moonlight bouncing off the frozen white rolling crusts threaten to break the quietude.

Pausing to contemplate a thick passage, the kind that takes more than a single read-through, I catch a faint mumble. It slowly enters my awareness, penetrating the silence – voices at a party muffled by distance or physical barriers. This humming beehive swarms without detail or distinguishable speech; nevertheless, my attention remains fixed on the vague murmur of human chattering.

I meet my new discovery with contemplation and cautious intrigue. Why? Because our residence sits within a typical suburban neighborhood, where rows of similar dwellings line quiet streets outside a small city. We live far enough from any infrastructure to save us from more concentrated light pollution and street noise. As such, after seven o'clock in the evening past fall, it's unlikely to hear anything but an occasional car door. Near the witching hour, deep within the winter...utter silence. In addition, the master bedroom looks out over our backyard and faces opposing houses over two hundred yards away. Homes on either side of us rest quite closely in contrast to the back. Still, a wide swath of ground buffers one family's dwelling from another. All that, yet I hear people – and lots of them. Even more strangely, the noise drifts in from the right corner of my bedroom. *The right corner of my bedroom?*

Now, curiosity entirely replaces reading, while I turn all focus to listen carefully. As my ears search for details in this strange encounter, the noise shifts. Dance music adds to the mix – a heavy-base-techno-vibe word-salad of sorts. *It's definitely a party*, I think out loud, whispering under my breath to only myself.

Frozen like an animal who stops to assess its environment, my ears strain, peaked to their utmost height while the rest of me barely breaths. My brain intentionally pauses for a millisecond – a deep dopamine-fueled inhale preparing for a frantic dive, a plunge into some Einsteinian abyss, looking for intelligent neural pathways filled with answers. My goal, neatly split between two opposing directions:

    1) Confirm this as a figment of my imagination;
    2) Let time reveal what gray matter can't understand.

I'm uncertain which is best.

Reluctantly, I slide out from the warm blankets, moving seemingly closer to the source of sound, and approach the back window. The heat from my breath makes a pale fog on the cold glass as I stare out into the night. *Who could be having a lawn party near midnight in the winter?*

Nobody, of course, answers the logical part of me.

Scanning as far as I can see, to the bare trees nearly engulfed by an inky sky, only silence meets me. Pure silence. Its evening dance partners – alternating gusts of wind and piercing white moonlight.

Not convinced, I look for lights...movement...any sign of activity to explain the mysterious party noise, but not a single glimmer shines through nearby windows. There's not even one person, let alone a party.

Glancing from house to house, yard to yard, I keep searching and thinking that evidence must somehow be evading me, but no – no parties here. Not even a peep.

Now, self-talk tries to quell my pale anxiety. "This must be something in the ethers or the astral plane. Then again, maybe...just maybe, I'm crazy!" An audible mumble escapes my lips and skips across the room, loud enough to momentarily disturb our younger dog, who steals a lazy peek.

Worry, instead of answers, drives me back to bed – an attempt to replace concern with warmth and hopefully sleep. *Maybe clarity will come tomorrow.*

There is no clarity. In the following days, music seems to follow me to the most unassuming of places, like a lost puppy seeking solace. Since that first "invisible party," etheric voices and faint melodies visit time and again with increasing frequency. They often become noticeable when I feel centered and still, especially in my master bedroom late at night. But more occurrences don't quell my concern about what I *really* hear and from where.

It's been weeks since the first mysterious midnight merrymaking, and I'm at another spiritual retreat, a break and respite from the world. Picture an old inn nestled deep within the New York mountains. Three stories of gently peeling white from years of layered paint rest between a funeral home and a real-estate business on the only main street through the center of town. I imagine it in another era, serving weary travelers who made their way from place to place.

It's late Saturday morning, and we are on a break between teachings. I sit quietly with my back to the window, waiting for our session to resume. The carpet's outdated geometry has me playfully occupied as my consciousness flits like a butterfly sampling flowers – first with the hum of conversations, then to the sound of cars traveling by our busy street-front meeting room, and finally to echoes of clanging in the nearby inn kitchen.

Despite all noise filtering into and floating about the space, another sound sharply catches my attention. *Good grief, there it is again!* A critical thought – one that tightly holds hands with old worry – sweeps away my playful fluttering and turns it into intense focus. Somehow the sweetness of warm toffee notes relaxes the critic in me.

Carried by this honeyed melody, I listen as it softly drifts behind the collection of other noise, weaving its way through my consciousness. And despite all obvious inter-ference, my ears remain tipped toward this altogether different sound until light anxiety washes over me, yet again. *How can I hear orchestral music mixed with all this other racquet? This is crazy!*

Still not trusting my previous assessment – etheric or astral music – I begin to think the worst. *Maybe this is it! Maybe, this music signals my dive into some inescapable abyss of psychosis!*

I need to ask. Now I feel thoroughly grateful as well as relieved to be at a retreat. Here, I trust others' answers much more than my own.

I turn to Rev. Penny, hoping to solicit her thoughts on the matter. *If anyone can shed some light, it's Penny,* or so I think.

Seeing that she's alone, I quietly seize the moment and motion to her, grabbing her attention for my own. (As a trusted guide and powerful psychic, Penny is much sought-after.) Sitting beside her, I feel the pressing need for answers mixed with an undeniable fear of what she might say. Nevertheless, this risk is worth taking – to fill a void born of mystery and contaminated by an ego that's diabolically thrilled to keep me scared. So, I study her kind face, framed in frosty-white curls and complimented by a lined milky complexion, and speak.

"Penny, I keep hearing voices and music in a certain place in my house. I also heard it today at the retreat. I don't hear it with my ears, the same as regular music, but I do 'hear' it. I know that. Am I going crazy?"

Penny's quiet resolve and kind eyes hold me in compassionate regard, absent of all judgment and grave concern. She remains devoid of the negative thoughts I have toward myself. "No, dear, you're not going crazy," she reassures me. "You hear etheric music and music of the Universe. I hear it, too, at times. There's one place I hear violins when I drive on a particular route. You know the Universe has its own music, too."

Sweeping relief! *Etheric music. Songs of the Universe. Phew!* A sense of clarity fills the space created by the unseen, a space once knotted with anxiety.

I can breathe again.

I so wish I hadn't dismissed my initial understanding. Another lesson in trust is undeniably afoot.

❖

This story happened over ten years ago, yet as I polish these words, the cosmos sings another symphony. It delivers a reminder of what rests beyond our five senses in an ever-changing and eclectic gift from the Universe. Tonight, it's wrapped in violin solos and musical mastery – a lovely and welcome visit. The cooing voice of quivering golden strings chants braided angelic chords too delicious to ignore. And like a beautiful bedtime story, heard while resting in the arms of a loving parent, this bewitching melody gently lulls me into a peaceful sleep.

Thank you, stars! Thank you, Milky Way! Thank you, Universe! I hear you, Father, in violins.

❖

Reflections

❖ *Have you ever experienced something beyond your ordinary five senses?*

❖ *How did it make you feel?*

❖ *Was it a source of reassurance to support your faith, or did it challenge your beliefs regarding life and the world?*

Faith in Ladybugs

You are the beautiful sunshine that naturally attracts precious little ladybugs.
- Marta Shumylo

Faith consists in believing when it is beyond the power of reason to believe.
- Voltaire

W e are ever in a state of creating, manifesting as a natural outpicturing of our innate power. Often, we do this unknowingly or without much thought.

Manifesting - putting our creative energy into action - occurs when we sustain our idea long enough to see it birthed. We constantly bring mental energy into some form or another through our conscious and subconscious intent.

Intent - thought, fueled by feelings and emotions.

Intention builds our personal world - the things we have or don't have, the situations we walk through, and the relationships in our life – as we create moment by moment, projecting our energy to unfold before us.

The mechanics of manifesting inform us on the how and why of what's present in our life. To understand them, we begin by examining where we invest our energy. In other words, where are our thoughts and emotions joined in perfect chorus? Are we singing the songs of woe (worry, strife, discouragement, and negativity), or are our melodies infused with love (forgiveness, abundance, understanding, respect, compassion, joy, and wisdom)?

Most likely, we operate with a combination of attitudes: a spectrum of reactions and responses to whatever happens in our world. Regardless, where we place our focus and energy inextricably links to manifesting by *our faith.* Our faith resides wherever we decide to put it – in things, in people, in Source, in worry, in love, in the Universe...

Because I, too, fall prey to the ego and worry, I decided to practice manifesting through consciously focusing my faith. Hatching a simple project that seemed fun and light, especially because no pressure existed to produce something attached to survival, I intended to manifest ladybugs.

Now I know you might think, how can anyone manifest ladybugs? Ladybugs live in the world; they come and go as they please and that's that. Well, using our creative powers, we can bring what we desire into our life. Our connection to the divinity in anything through love sets the energy in motion. And yes, we can use that energy to serve the purpose of bringing ladybugs or various other critters to visit us.

❖

Late in the winter, while ladybugs slumber, hidden from searching eyes, my plan seems to be an exciting experiment. I love ladybugs and always have, especially the symbolism of these creatures heralding a time of abundance and fulfillment of desires; even their tiny decorative black marks indicate something valuable – the number of gifts coming to us. Knowing the wide variation in ladybug markings, I began to wonder what the Universe would provide. *Maybe twelve or nine or seven gifts...great numbers*, I think, on a happy short walk to meditation.

The morning sun leaves dappled footprints across the tan carpet in my sacred space and gently comes to rest on my emerald green plant family, decorating their rich foliage. Sitting quietly for a moment before entering that peaceful place within me, I let a few deep breaths pave my path, washing away any feelings of hustle and urgency. As I ask my mind's eye to open, a meditation gift unfolds: the image of a ladybug in all her cerise glory. The beautiful red crest of her back, dotted with perfect black specks, contrasts her bright white "eyes."

My heart connects with love and affection for this tiny crimson jewel, and I expand the vision to call in ladybugs everywhere. Imagination paints beautiful pictures, and I "see" ladybugs on walls and windows, sprinkled on pages in books, adorning cards, and decorating lapels as jewelry. Here, mind and heart merge into a *knowing – a deep feeling of crystal-clear possibility* (faith in action), graced with a grand ladybug deluge...as sure as a small child's faith in Santa's special delivery under the Christmas tree...as certain in the sun filling the sky.

My heartfelt gratitude and love for these little creatures permeate a consciousness beyond thought; I believe in and feel the power within me. Through faith in my Higher Self, I release expectations on any exact outcomes while holding to the original feeling-thought manifesting power and opening to the Universe's work.

Two days pass before the first signs of my project appear, a bejeweled friend pinned to a sweater – a courier dressed in red and black paint, not breathing, but a sign nonetheless. I thank the Universe and stay watchful.

Later that afternoon, a live version lands on my jacket. Like a kid on a treasure hunt, I smile ear to ear with ladybug fever!

The next day, fifteen ladybugs gather in the sunshine inside my patio window, the world unfolding by my request. A serendipitous, cosmic smile – seventeen bugs total align with seventeen spots on two scarlet gems I paused to count.

I rest in the number and its symbolism:

> **One** – the power of oneness and unity; and
> **Seven** – spiritual consummation; movement into a higher, wiser order.

Learning how to consciously manifest in our lives is a valuable and powerful lesson. Truth dictates that we continually create and manifest, if not from our clear, conscious intentions, then from a mindset that lurks below the surface, hidden but compelling. So, attention to all that shows its face in our life holds the key to understanding what we manifest moment by moment.

You see, the key to change in your life, in the world, is *YOU. You make the difference.* You hold more power than your brain can imagine. Yes, little old you can have the life you desire. You can be a beacon of light: light is your core.

You, the Whole You, are a vessel of love, light, and goodness. Every loving thought, every act of compassion, every forgiveness, every kindness radiates from you into your world to affect everything and everyone, *especially you.* Remember, we are One, and any changes in your life ripple out in ever-increasing circles to bless your world.

Yes, Child of the Universe, the world is at your finger-tips. Go out there and get those ladybugs![16]

---

[16] Revised from Adriene Nicastro, *The Soul-Discovery Journalbook: An Intimate Journey into Self, Volume III, Faith in Ladybugs,* (Bellefonte, PA: Pathways to Freedom Press, 2021), pp. 293-298.

Reflections

❖ *What have you manifested in your life lately?*

❖ *Was it a desired or an unwanted manifestation? Why?*

❖ *What might you change about your attitude regarding situations, events, or possessions in your life?*

❖ *How might these changes alter the manifesting energy you use to create?*

❖ *What would the changes mean for you?*

The Spot

We are what our thoughts have made us:
so take care about what you think.
Words are secondary.
Thoughts live; they travel far.
~ Swami Vivekananda

We often associate manifesting with monetary abundance and the things it can buy – lovely homes, sparkly trinkets, handsome cars, and such. But expanding our minds beyond the birthing of stuff, we can witness the beauty of creation to understand our God-given abilities in so many more realms. For example, consider the people, situations, events, and gifts of learning that grace our presence. Here, manifesting offers opportunities in love and support as well as the more difficult exercises in boundaries and forgiveness. It even includes our physical wellbeing or illnesses that we experience.

Now, I know what you're thinking. How can I manifest what seems to be so beyond my control? Well, truth is, our world happens *through us, not to us*. In other words, our life is like a movie, projected through our video-player self to demonstrate our attitudes and beliefs via the Emmy-winning stories that make up our personal world. You live out situations, events, and lessons *created* by…yup, you guessed it…you!

Perhaps, being the scriptwriter of your life's stores, the "out-there" events we face, make sense. But manifesting health or illness? That often feels more elusive, our bodies doing what they will without our consent. In the metaphysical realm, however, wellbeing and disease are never as they appear. In fact, they take on a whole new meaning. Specifically, wellness, illness, physical pain, and injury demonstrate how we see ourselves or our world, symbolized by the body system or part affected. Our health, then, repeats the tale of manifesting – our internal climate displayed in a metaphorical way. This is the story of my spot, a humorous saga of manifesting in action.

I have manifested a spot, a giant paper-bag-brown freckle that sits squarely on my upper cheekbone, almost sha-dowed by my long eyelashes. In fact, it nearly looks like a second eyeball, tricking onlookers into focusing and refocusing as they try to figure out which one is real.

OK, that's a bit dramatic and not totally true, so scratch that.

The spot is distracting *to me,* and day after day, it draws my attention. The amount it generates is quite astound-ing, energy I could spend elsewhere. Annoyingly, it's a potent distraction I can't escape.

Some days my spot mimics a zit with impeccable timing: the kind that arrives squarely on your forehead just before an important event. You know, the obnoxious wedding crashers that could ruin a perfectly nice day. Ugh!

To demonstrate my point, I'll give this spot a name. It feels big enough for that. I'll call it... Frankie. Of course, a boy, because females have better sense than to show up like that, and because he's on the right side of my face, my symbolically masculine side according to metaphysical references.

Frankie must go! I'm too young for a giant age spot on my face! Age spots are for eighty-year-olds, cries the beauty-driven script in my head. These thoughts echo through my brain harkening to a childhood mindset, a daily mantra dripping with self-judgment and worry.

Today's the day, I tell myself, the beginning of systematically getting rid of Frankie. I'll call it Frankie's Relocation Program. Subtitle: Goodbye Frankie! Bon voyage!

Sayonara, sucker! The thirteen-year-old in me snickers.

When I started the relocation program, looking for reasons to explain Frankie's arrival became paramount. Now, it's clear, the obvious culprit shining in my eyes – the sun. So, as each day begins, I race to the master bathroom, a frantic sprint dedicated to slathering mineral-based sunscreen on Frankie before a single photon of light can sneak through the upstairs windows. This morning, again, I squirt the standard pea-sized pearl of miracle cream on the tip of my finger, slathering it like butter on a bagel and think, *Bye-bye brown guy! I've got your number.*

Weeks have passed, and no matter how completely I cover Frankie in that Frankenstein-white paste, he continues to grow. The goodbye party is down the drain.

Each morning he stares back at me with contempt and stubbornness. I hate him, and in turn he haunts me, showing up everywhere I go. Look in the mirror and there he is. Back up the car and uh-oh, rear-view reflections. Clothes shopping, haircuts, store-front windows, family photos, Skype. *Ugh!* Clearly, he mocks me, representing age and imperfection, a swear word from old family messages that hold flawless beauty in high regard.

Sorry, Frankie. You're a flaw. A defect. A smudge. You're making me crazy and, dare I say...making me more imperfect than ever!

Frankie really must have a pea-brain all his own. The more I focus on him, the faster he grows. I can't seem to stop the spread of his amebic, milk-chocolate body. Today... today is the worst of all! A disturbing change seems to signal danger; no longer flat, Frankie has fattened up like he's been sneaking midnight manicotti. Elevated and more irregular, he just issued a dangerous threat. Right under my watchful right eye (literally) lay a mini mob boss. The extortion – unbearable.

Watching friends, neighbors, and relatives suffer from cancerous skin lesions, all I can think about is Frankie and how I will meet his demands. What is it he wants? I can't bear the thought of living with him or the added complications of disease eating away at my face. *This relocation program has failed for sure!*

Frankie and I are out for the afternoon. I bring him to a lunch date to meet a friend. While he lazily naps, I complain tactlessly behind his back.

"I can't stand this spot!" I gesture with an angry finger toward Frankie and my right eye. "It's driving me positively crazy! Look!" I stretch my neck awkwardly forward to emphasize my point, like some strange homage to the Chicken Dance (missing wing-flapping and butt-bumping, of course).

Jackie slides her reading glasses onto her nose, and all I can think is, *Seriously, you can't possibly need those!* Perhaps she's trying to assure me that she has taken this problem earnestly – or worst, maybe she's mocking me?

I'm not quite sure, but then she thoughtfully advises. "You'd better start loving that spot or you're guaranteeing a trip to the dermatologist!"

Love Frankie? Seriously? How could I love this little monster? (Pause, wheels turning...)

Yes, of course! Love Frankie. What a gift! I became so negatively focused on him, the basic spiritual premise of manifesting through belief eluded me. All my energy fixated on despising him, creating the perfect Frankie to hate.

I change my mind, Frankie! Forget the old plan. My new journey: Frankie Forgiveness.

Frankie Forgiveness is in full swing. I see him differently now. When he pops into the mirror, I wave and say hi with affection. I greet him with warmth in the car mirror. As I put on mascara, I give the blind guy eyes and a mouth, a token of humorous recognition. (Not really, but it's tempting.) More importantly, I intentionally offer myself healthy approval. Curbing the initial curling lip of distaste, my focus shifts to other endeavors. Steadfast on this journey, I refuse to allow Frankie's presence to disrupt my day. *I see you, Frankie. Have a good afternoon!*

It's been over two months now, accepting my little friend, accepting myself, loving him, and embracing his presence. This is Frankie Forgiveness in action. And guess what? He packed his capicola-loving carcass and completely disappeared without a trace – no dermatologist or special treatment – just a turn in perceptions and voila! *Thank you, Frankie!*

Now, I'm not negating medical treatment or affirming some lack of value in it. If Frankie started packing on severe, morbid weight instead of making a timely exit, my course of action would have included a doctor (or maybe even a bigger mobster – not sure). Clearly, though, changing the thoughts, feelings, and beliefs about my appearance helped me recognize that Frankie was only trying to help. He really did want me to be happy, after all. Happy and loving toward myself with or without him. *Bon voyage, buddy! Guess the original plan worked anyway!*

Years later, I can say...Thanks, Frankie! You arrived in perfect timing. I think of you fondly now, and for old time's sake, I'll say hi for you to your thirty-seven little cousins who moved in during menopause. Thanks again for the lesson in self-love.[17]

---

[17] **Summary:** Frankie manifested on the right side of my face, representing how I thought men viewed me, a fear regarding my projected perceptions about getting older and reinforced through relationships during Frankie's birth.

Body Symbolism:

Face – represents the part of us shown to the world.

Skin – represents the protective barrier between us and the world; how we feel about ourselves or others shows on our skin, especially the attitudes/beliefs we may not be able to speak out loud.

Age spots– represent a feeling of aging or seeing ourselves as old.

Right side – represents the masculine side of our body; our relationships with men, our father, and our action/doing self.

Left side – represents the feminine side of our body; our relationship with women, our mother, and our nurturing/ live-giving self.

For more information on healing and metaphysical symbolism, see *Healing: Select Lessons of Archangel Gabriel* by Rev. Penny Donovan.

❖

Reflections

❖ *What lessons in self-love have crossed your path? Is there an aspect of you that requires your acceptance?*

❖ *Are there attributes of your physical form that could be responding to your attitudes in a way that you don't like or want, creating a self-fulfilling prophecy?*

❖ *How might you benefit from changing your mind about those attributes or yourself to cultivate more self-love and acceptance?*

Fairy Dreams

Come Fairies, take me out of this dull world,
for I would ride with you upon the wind
and dance upon the mountains like a flame!
~ William Butler Yeats

I've been fascinated by fairies since I was a child. Tinker Bell, Cinderella's Fairy God-mothers, and the tiny-winged companions of Sleeping Beauty were the more famous and mesmerizing cast of characters I longed to meet.

Unlike what you may think, fairies don't just belong to the famed Walt Disney who borrowed these magical creatures from the annals of mythological history, arche-typal tales, and European storybooks. Actively living in the hearts of many cultures, fairies, gnomes, leprechauns, and other enchanted entities weave their way through folklore and daily life. The Irish, for example, dedicate parks and special landscapes to them. Regular sightings are quite common there. In Scandinavia, we find elves and trolls, which made their way into Sunday's after-dinner tales – fond memories of my Swedish paternal step-grandmother.

As we travel to America, however, fairy folk and their friends live mostly in cartoons and the imaginary realms of children's books and fantasy novels. But if we dare enter the metaphysical, New Age spirituality, or Wiccan faiths, a door to the fairy world opens, and a whole new dimension reveals its secrets.

Actively studying metaphysical and spiritual materials, I discovered how teachings on fairies, gnomes, sprites, and elementals come with the territory. So, even though I dropped fairies in the proverbial toy box along with other fanciful imaginings of my bright-eyed, platinum-topped inner child, I had a new opportunity to meet my old friends. For some reason, though, I didn't take too much stock in the literature I found, even from my most treasured Sacred Garden Fellowship lectures. Perhaps my adult self took over, feeling skeptical regardless of dedicated spiritual study and expanded beliefs. Or maybe, I, too, adopted the standard American mindset, relegating fairies to make-believe.

Whatever the reason, I eventually found great comfort in the supposed fantastical, especially when viewed through a spiritual lens. That said, I still operate with discernment when sharing the matter. Why, you ask? Because to let fairy-loving, fairy-believing talk sneak out of the proverbial closet in particular company could be rather uncomfortable. Mention to your average person that you *really* believe in fairies and watch for a contemptuous eye-roll or quick change of topic. It may even get you a special delivery of little blue pills dedicated to making the little buggers "disappear" forever.

So, long ago I decided that it's just not a wise conversation piece if I want to avoid negative judgment, keep friends, or dodge pharmacological trouble with anyone carrying a prescription pad. Despite these concerns, I offer what I've learned, and you can decide for yourself. (And if you stop talking to me in the months to come, I might know why.)

Fairies, gnomes, sprites, leprechauns, and dwarves, also called elementals, are part of the angelic life-force. Specifically, they are the angels, known as Devas, that aid plants, flowers, trees, mineral life, and animals. Because Source created angels for every lifeform in existence, each living being[18] has Devas – angels that serve, guard, and guide in a way specific to the species or manifestation.

We can attune to elemental energy by raising our vibration to match Deva frequencies. Through psychic or intuitive work, a beautifully magical union unfolds, "seeing" them in our third-eye space, "hearing" them, or sensing their presence. If we're particularly psychic or live somewhere they're welcomed and accepted, we may even see them objectively. Yet, regardless of how or where, Devas are an energy made of light, absent a corporeal existence, and will appear in ways that resonate with us, unique to the person making the connection.

After years of study, I can tune into the different energies of elementals. Most of all, though, I find myself intrigued with fairies. It's in this way that the child in me lives on, I suppose.

Uncertain of exactly what draws me, anything that attempts to capture their essence and dainty form becomes eye-catching and alluring. Maybe, too, it stems

---

[18] Living entities include rocks and minerals despite most people considering them as non-living. Made of God-substance, just as you and I, rocks and mineral life have a unique consciousness all their own, each emanating a specific vibration beneficial for healing.

from a love of butterflies and other delicately winged gifts from nature. Attempting to precisely pinpoint the reason seems irrelevant, now. I just love fairies to pieces, so much so that a deep longing began to press on my consciousness. And so, the story goes...

It's spring and the draw to a forest landscape tugs potently at my heart. So, I give in to the pull and find myself deep in the woods of Tussey Mountain. I feel more connected and in tune with my winged friends here than I used to, and part of me hopes that today's hike helps the fairies emerge from the shadows.

Any of us who've studied the metaphysical, Druidic, or Wicca teachings know that wooded landscapes hold blessed opportunities to connect with Devas. Nested in the glory of their natural habitat, they relish sacred space away from most humans.

Stopping momentarily by a nearby shallow stream, I look across the rich feathery ferns and imagine a fairy sitting on a rock as another hides under a red speckled toadstool. Perhaps one will pelt me with an acorn or stand coyly in a single ray of sunlight, begging notice.

Pressing into congregating families of tree friends, I walk deeper into the land. A palpable energetic shift comes to my awareness. The fairy vibrations – at least as I experience them – permeate the space. They feel distinctly different from other elementals, and though I cannot pinpoint concrete evidence, a buoyant and cheerful ambiance infuses the ethers, like a hint of honeysuckle on a gentle spring breeze.

Dwarves and gnomes feel earthier – heavier and intently protective. Unlike the fairies, they hide in thick patches of underbrush, camouflaged in tracks of fallen porcupine trees whose broken branches stand erect in spiked warnings. I smile, remembering them, especially the "feeling" of their invisible KEEP OUT signs in the last glen.

At a bend in the streambed, shimmering waves of cheerful chartreuse grass pool in glowing clusters under honey beams of light. Painting everything in rich green velvet, moss keeps the shallow banks company, fuzzy lime that pours across water-worn sculptures – haphazardly strewn rocks that offer structure and form to the stream's wet burping and chuckling. *If only I were small enough to tiptoe there and sit, a tiny mouse with careful, petal-soft footsteps.*

A hushed prayer forms on my lips from a most heartfelt space. *Please, let me see you.* It's accompanied, perhaps, by the subtle sense that I am not alone. In my mind the fairy-folk dance in joy-filled parties. They lounge, ever so delicately, on Mother Nature's furry-green carpets, drinking dew from bluebell flowers while giggling and chatting.

My intense longing to know them, to see them, grows and grows, a palpable ache in my heart. The sunshine of my soul warms this seed, which sprouts happily and stretches toward the light. Now, I wait patiently for gestational gifts to spring forth. But despite my longing, not a single fairy has jumped out of their leafy home to say, "Hello!" Weeks later, something altogether unexpected did…

❖

It's a very lovely spring afternoon, the kind that calls for reading in deliciously relaxing spots, those soaked by the sun and filled with furry pets and fluffy blankets. For me, this spot is bed stacked with copious amounts of books. To set the record straight, not even one is a fantasy novel, unlike what you might think. Instead, studying, absorbing, and sifting through spiritual material is this afternoon's pleasure, the kind that speaks to the most amazing truth – words that feed my soul.

Reading and relaxing just happens to be a luscious recipe for sleep – sleep and beautiful dreams. So, with heavy eyelids, I close my book and eyes.[19]

Floating, my consciousness drifts. A lucid dream – the inner mindscape halfway between fully awake and completely asleep – provides a lovely space of peace. As a pleasant warmth floods in, like gentle heat from bathwater, it softly surrounds my form: skin, limbs, face, and head all gently wrapped.

A vision gradually takes shape, painted in pinkish-yellow sunlight. Soft and rich, like a blurred impressionistic landscape, focus slowly defines the space with curious figures suspended by paper-thin wings. These beautiful creatures dance in a sea of blushing gold and whipped luminescent papaya while their lovely features shine with the most exquisite perfection, flawless little faces sweetly looking back at me. Tiny graceful bodies with the most

---

[19] As a note of context, I've dreamt in colors for as long as I can remember with vivid colors and intense detail – all senses blooming in textures, smells, tactile sensations, and sounds. I thought everyone had dreams like this, but now I know this is part of being empathic. See *An Empath's Checklist*

refined detail – petite toes, gently curving calves, slender arms, and fingers – complement an altogether sinewy frame of living art. Iridescent butterfly wings in velvety-soft, orange-scarlet, stained-glass poetry suspend flying, miniature ballerinas, who flutter delicately to keep themselves afloat. Hovering around me, their love smiles in giggling, wing-flapping glory, radiating light from the most elegant, opalescent, rosy-bronze-gold skin – a divine amalgam, indeed.

I, too, feel suspended, completely mesmerized.

How magnificent! How striking! Perfect. Gorgeous. Stunning. These are the echoes in my heart – a mantra that chants labels insufficient to all I see. Taken over by their splendor and unconditional love, tears stream down my face. *You're so beautiful!* Silent words whisper prayers not quite formed on barely-sleeping lips, but offered, nonetheless. I feel enveloped, completely held – a babe safe in mother's loving arms.

I so want to stay here with them, wherever here is, somewhere between the astral plane and corporeal consciousness. So, I mentally clinging to the vision. *Please stay! Don't leave!* I beg, longing to live there forever.

I fight my descent to earth, to bed, and to my tear-stained pillow, but it's futile. They fade, one precious detail at a time until there's nothing but blackness. Being awake brings such bittersweet aching – a feeling of longing mixed with lingering comfort and companionship. Enveloped in a symphony, a masterpiece of Divine Grace, I feel full. Full with love and gratitude. Kissed by fairy-love, drunk on a bliss-cocktail of radiance and joy. When I desire, I have a place to return to, a vision to remember, a space in my heart painted in beauty.

The sweetest feelings of these magical friends still linger in my fondest memories. A gift, a treasure, a reassurance of life beyond our small, three-dimensional world. Words feel inadequate to describe my fairy dreams.

I want to tell the world, to shout their joy-filled visit from the highest mountain, but I won't. This chapter, for now, is as close as I get. So, consider yourself lucky. Even though evidence of my fairy life lies within these pages, you'll rarely hear me talk about them, just in case someone with a prescription pad lurks in the shadows, pushing little blue pills.

❖

Reflections

❖ *What are your feelings and beliefs about angels, fairies, and other elemental energies?*

❖ *Have you had any experiences with them? Sensed their energy?*

❖ *What adventures could open the door to angels, fairies, or other elementals?*

The Shell

*Those who look for seashells will find seashells;
those who open them will find pearls.*

~ Imam Al-Ghazali

hile I've given spiritual readings, speaking to Divine helpers and passed over loved ones, I primarily use intuitive skills and spirit communication to enhance my therapeutic sessions. This work helps uncover the blockages clients encounter on their journeys or gives me insight into interventions. As such, some people arrive at my door for counseling, others for psycho-spiritual therapy, and some for spiritual healing as energy work combined with Spirit-directed guidance. That said, helping others is what I love, born of a deep desire to aid those on their path of personal evolution.

Even though I endeavor to be open, non-judgmental, and unhindered by personality, doing psycho-spiritual work as a healer can still bring on a bout of expectations. In fact, throughout our relationships, whether we're helping or just socializing, the nature of humans is to conjure expectations of how any experience "should" unfold. It's a way for us to predict outcomes or attempt to control an endpoint. At other times, we may look for some benchmark to evaluate ourselves, assessing how well we did or didn't do. Used constructively, this can work in our favor, but when self-judgments come knocking, overt and even covert expectations may sabotage our progress.

Because I, too, fall prey to expectations, I must employ vigilance to navigate the beliefs that sustain them. Consistent observance is especially essential when I work with clients, holding sessions that call for tuning in to Divine Presence.

Within the realm of psycho-spiritual work, spiritual readings, and intuitive messages, the Universe calls us to intentionally move *with* Spirit. As such, raising our vibration beyond expected outcomes allows us to offer clear wisdom and guidance. The human brain, however, loves to get in the way of this flow – to manufacture ideas of what the information means or how helpful it will be. However, when we are present with Spirit and allow, magic happens, and what unfolds becomes more of a miracle than our little minds can ever imagine.

One such spiritual reading stands out in my mind, more memorable than it initially appeared – another lesson to be mindful of expectations and perceptions. My dear friend (and soul sister) Vanya, searching for a meaning-ful and healing present for her sister Sasha, surprised her with a spiritual reading from…yes, you guessed it, me. This special exchange from sister to sister, born of intentions for clarity and understanding, growth and development, was delivered for Sasha's birthday.

As many spiritual readings go, the typical themes – life passion, desires, talents, and so on – played an important part in my meeting with Sasha; however, these details vanished from my consciousness soon after the reading ended, the case with most of these healing sessions. One impression, though, remained comfortably in my memory – a visit from Sasha's angel, who entered the reading in the very first moments we connected. Here's how the experience wove its magic.

"Sasha, your angel has something for you," I said, describing what I saw.

Resting in the palm of her angel's luminous hand lay a beautiful white shell, the kind that looked like a miniature conch but with delicate, smooth walls. I drew the shell for Sasha...

"Your angel offers it as a gift. You'll know it when the time comes."

Nothing more was forthcoming with the message. Funny thing, though, Sasha had plans to travel. The following week, she would join Vanya on a trip to Hawaii. A message about an angel giving her a shell seemed about as significant as a vision about a french-fry vendor handing out ketchup packets. *So what?!*

After the sisters' Hawaii trip, I receive a call from Vanya, recanting tales from their journey on the island of Kauai.

Later in another lively call with them both, we relive their magical adventure and the highlights from their trek on the famous Kalalau Trail.

I know nothing about the Kalalau Trail, which sounds rather innocuous at first. Island, hiking, beach, beauty… what can be better than this heavenly combination? Those perceptions, however, quickly shift after some timely research.

The Kalalau Trail happens to be one of the ten most dangerous hikes *in the world*.[20] (Ok, I'm paying attention, now!) A daring eleven miles one way, its treacherous path collects a myriad of "no's" – no cell service, no nearby inhabitants, no organized rests along the way, frequently no other hikers, and no legal or safe end-point. On the other hand, it flaunts jagged lava rocks, narrow and tangled tropical footpaths, numerous jungle wildlife (both innocuous and dangerous), and multiple drop-offs, hundreds of feet above a bouldered shoreline. One carelessly planted step can be deadly – an end, sadly, many travelers have faced.

Young and adventurous, inexperienced, and perhaps even foolish, Sasha and Vanya set out to travel the Kalalau Trail in its entirety. Their only plan – a one-way journey ending in an illegal boat ride – was a delicately timed rendezvous at the beach after their eleven-mile jaunt. That, combined

---

[20] The Kalalau Trail has been the cause of multiple fatalities and countless other close calls. At the Hanakapi'ai Falls, adjoining the trail, there have been eight deaths, and in the waters off Hanakapi'ai beach, at the trail's end, nearly 100 fatalities occurred due to treacherous currents. At the beginning of 2019, the state of Hawaii indefinitely closed the Kalalau Trail after a lawsuit over one man's death and multiple search and rescue calls signaled a need for action. The trail reopened, but in 2020 officials reported an additional fatality. Accurate numbers appear difficult to ascertain.

with the return to their comfortable hotel, became the necessary bookends to keep their escapade as manageable as possible.

Miles and miles of boiling heat, humid air, twisted landscapes, and dangerous drop-offs quickly, however, become formidable adversaries. Light sandals, Vanya's personal enemy, created swollen and blistered ankles and feet. She hoped this painful burden would end by the time they reached the beach.

Then another barrier arose, a deadly narrow cliff hundreds of feet above the ocean. The young women needed to navigate these jagged rocks with no foothold or line of sight around a corner, where the path disappeared into an abyss. How could they move around an edge without seeing where to step?

Overcome with fear and unsure of how to literally move forward, Sasha and Vanya felt trapped and terrified. Their boat would be waiting on the beach, but how could they find their way there, especially around this sinister turn in the trail?

Well, Divine design never fails to intervene! A seasoned traveler, Leilani, was a local, quite familiar with the trail. She miraculously appeared, the only other hiker on the entire path, to guide Vanya and Sasha through the steepest, most treacherous scramble, around the blind edge, and down the mountainous cliff-face. Sasha followed Leilana, an earth angel full of courage, confidence, and surefootedness. She inspired Sasha, who mimicked her step-by-step. Then, seeing Vanya's tormented feet, Leilana offered her hiking shoes. Was it any surprise that they fit her perfectly?

❖

The two sisters arrived at the end of their descent on the sandy shore – blistered, sore, swollen, and exhausted, but in one piece.

"It was way more difficult than I thought. So dangerous, too," reported Vanya. "But we made it! Then the bad news...the boat's captain, arrested for illegally transporting hikers from the trail, landed in jail. There would be no boat; no transport back, unless we called a rescue helicopter!"

Their only solution: hike the eleven miles back and return to the entry point. There was just no other way.

Aching and exhausted, Vanya and Sasha stayed that night on the beach, visiting with a tiny handful of others camping on the island: a mix of locals and vagabonds in a free-spirited community permanently in residence. Bathing in the magical energy and untouched landscape, they decided to plan their upcoming return after some rest and food. Both knew what was in store for them, and neither welcomed it.

"I knew I had to do something differently. We couldn't make it back drowning in our all-consuming fear. So, I drew on every spiritual tool I could think of," Vanya explained. "Praying, meditating, centering, calling on the angels, my confidence and sense of protection returned, but Sasha...she was in a whole other place. Then I remembered something Stella[21] said to me. '*Anything is*

---

[21] Stella is a Master Teacher channeled through Rev. Penny Donovan.

as difficult as you expect it to be.' And so I knew that shifting my expectations was really important."

"I couldn't do it," recounts Sasha. "Fear just took over – paralyzing fear. I kept saying, 'I'm not doing it. I'm gonna die. I'll slip and fall down that cliff.' Then, I felt bad. I was supposed to be the confident big sister, and I was terrified."

After a talk, a morning pep rally led by Vanya about all their Divine help, the sisters set out again – back the eleven miles. With her newfound shoes, Vanya stepped more sure-footedly, but leftover discomfort and soreness, made her wonder about the long, steep path. How would this treacherous trail meet her and she it?

Sasha, still drenched in dread, fretted about the most dangerous passage – the three-hundred-foot drop-off around the blind corner, perched above a threatening rocky shoreline. One heartfelt reminder about Divine help just wasn't enough, and questions continued to press heavily on her. Most of all, she thought, how will we climb up what was so perilous coming down?

Although the sisters truly desired to stay in tune with Spirit, they were raw, weary, and palpably aware of being without help – without human help, that is. As a result, Sasha continued to anticipate disaster, like a fat-footed giant made to walk a fragile, thin wire. Standing on the path awash with intense anxiety and uncertainty, she looked back at Vanya. As emotions surged through Sasha, an oh-my-God-here-we-go feeling reached into every cell. Unable to conceal the panic, it registered on her face, painting Sasha in utter anguish.

Seeing her sister's expression, Vanya continued to cheer them on. She reminded Sasha and herself of all their

Divine assistance with a we-got-this, we're-protected attitude. She hoped her faith would rub off on Sasha, even if only for a brief time.

Preparing to trudge onward, both paused, looking skyward to the steepest rocky cliff-face. It finally, but ominously lay before them. And so, with a deep-breath beginning, the women started their scramble.

One inch at a time, Sasha and Vanya made their ascent, navigating up the rough, gravelly bluff. Keeping their sights immediately ahead on the steep incline, they attempted to leave behind any thoughts about the growing distance between them and flat ground.

It's funny how time collapses when our focus becomes finely sculpted to a razor's edge – this in carefully planted hands and feet, the four-limbed clamber up the rocky cliff. Ants on a tall bumpy monster.

Suddenly, climbing up, surrounded by monotone debris, something unexpectedly caught Sasha's eye and made her pause. A white shell, resting in plain view, sat quietly, perched all alone. Curiously, its solitary post rested hundreds of feet above the ocean, surrounded only by charcoal-gray lava rocks and other non-descript stones. Sasha excitedly scooped the little beauty from its pebbled bed and held it out for Vanya to see.

"This is the shell! The shell from the reading...the one the angel handed me! It's exactly like the drawing Adriene made!"

Gasping, with a mix of emotions, everything spontaneously shifted for Sasha. She immediately felt a sense of peace. The overpowering fear that consumed her every step lifted away, profoundly and a sense of lightness, freedom, and intimate protection took its place.

"I felt like the angels were holding my arm, an energy that stayed through the rest of the hike," recounted Sasha.

For Vanya, all the angelic forces she called upon suddenly became illuminated through material reassurance. "We were so carried...so uplifted and joyful," remembered Vanya. "The potency of finding that shell, knowing it was a gift and feeling the shift that came with it. Priceless!"

Both sisters welcomed the happy surprise – a journey transformed. They continued, now in joy, a sense of cheerful adventure. Even Vanya's feet were recovering and more comfortable in her gifted shoes.

Still more incredible, the ease with which they traveled through the dangerous passage had them second-guess their location. "Did we already navigate that dreaded drop-off? Maybe it's coming up? That was so easy. That couldn't be it. Could it!?"

They realized that, indeed, the most treacherous part of their climb was over. And just as exciting, the shell from the reading was now clear. Sasha's angel had lovingly unveiled a timely nautical offering – a reminder of guidance, protection, and care.

In divine timing, miracles continued for the rest of the hike. Traveling through the jungle, they met an adorable wild baby boar, navigated by moonlight effortlessly, found safe shelter from torrential rainfall in the depth of the night, and securely camped on the dense tropical forest floor.

Through sacred symbolism, Sasha and Vanya came to see Cosmic influences all around them:

Kauai – called the womb of the world; this island boasts seven energy centers that mirror our body's seven chakras (spiritual energy points of evolution).

Ocean – represent emotions; Divine Feminine; mother and mother energy; psychic energy through the water element; connection with our intuitive side or the voice of Source within us.

Island – represents isolation from society; our relationship to rules, mores, and social boundaries; our ego's (or little self's) relationship to the unconscious, which in this case is the ocean.

Feet – represent understanding; the opening to an awareness of a truth within; moving forward and the accompanying attitude.

Cliff/Bluff – represents anxiety; fear of the unknown; taking a risk.

Mountain – represents obstacles; the spiritual or intellectual "rising" or improvement that comes with traveling them.

Wild boar – represents the need or desire to embrace and live life with adventure, joy, playfulness, and love; identifies a need to get away from the world and into nature; symbolizes protection and defense; mother energy that demonstrates nurturing, love, and care.

Cone shell – represents protection.

Ultimately, the sisters came *to know* themselves – an embodiment of the Divine Feminine, intimately guided, eternally protected, and deeply in tune – connected to self and Self through Mother Earth. Growth, trust, fearlessness, divine safety, joy, understanding: these are the themes of one miraculous quest, a journey in faith. Two brave souls surrendered to their internal power, beyond expectations, and moved in Divine flow, a theme resonant to how this chapter began.

Spirit offerings are bountiful: mysteriously impactful, awe-inspiring, radiantly grace-filled, humbling blessings to behold. Sometimes, feedback from others can make the experience feel more valid, especially when our ego tells us otherwise. And when confirmation is for our highest good, we will receive it. Mostly, however, we must trust and let go of our expectations, remembering that Spirit and all expressions of Divine Design never fail to deliver – to nurture, teach, and shine the way.

I dare say Vanya, Sasha, and I all found potent messages on this journey! Thank you, ladies! Thank you, angels! Thank you, Higher Self! Thank you, Spirit! We hear you. And we are blessed, indeed.

❖

Reflections

❖ What adventures might you explore symbolically to understand the hidden gifts they hold?

❖ How have expectations taken you out of the moment or altered how you experience a journey or event in your life?

❖ What expectations would be helpful to let go of and why?

❖ Have you ever consciously experienced the gifts of Spirit? What were they and how did they arrive?

❖ How might you focus more attention on what Spirit shows you in your life?

Artful Grasp

...and her heart opened with a twist.
The small silver key he gently held in an
artful grasp unlocked a lovely garden.
where each delicate bloom
revealed a treasure. He breathed in the sweetness.
abiding there in all that lay before him.
~ Adriene Nicastro

Love affairs and romances possess a magical quality all their own. The electric energy that pulls us to union ignites passion, desire, and connection. At times, what we experience takes us by surprise, on a mystical ride of euphoria, an unexpected visit from what appears as an outside force. A delivery from the unseen.

I met Dimitri in 2008 at my first spiritual retreat. This tall, shy bachelor studied mysticism, metaphysics, and spirituality in an alternate life – a covert endeavor intentionally apart from his daytime career and one we held in common. An easy conversationalist, his consistently soft demeanor offered a safe zone in my recovery from a challenging marriage and chaotic divorce.

Casual and comfortable in each other's presence, Dimitri and I stayed in touch via phone to span the days between retreats and the long miles from Pennsylvania to Vermont, where we respectfully lived. We compared notes, shared spiritual triumphs and challenges, and made an easy transition into friendship.

Anyone might say our connection built so slowly and steadily that eventually romance merely appeared to sneak up on us, stealth-like and coy. That's not how it happened for me, though. My feelings for Dimitri came more like a lightning bolt, a metaphysical experience equally balanced between the unexpected and the undeniable.

It's the fall of 2010, and Dimitri and I see one another, again, at a retreat. Like many retreats, joining with a healing partner during meditation is quite common, and so I ask if he wants to pair up for healing. His answer, predictable – a happy "yes" and an easy place where both of us can meet.

Taking each other's hands, we make a heartfelt, energetic connection – two friends ardently intent on being a conduit for sacred energy. A deep, cleansing breath helps me relax into a space within myself, a consciousness where sacred union, stillness, and higher vibrations converge.

At first, the black behind my closed eyes begins its usual shifts, movement in my third eye. Slowly, the darkness creates inky borders that run in stark contrast to a pulsating orange and green center. Part of me stays peacefully present, just observing.

Time fades, sitting beyond my awareness. Here, I float in a comforting river of energy...

Without warning, a vivid vision breaks with crisp clarity: rust-colored, rocky canyons with red, wind-sculpted stones stand so tall they engulf me. My mind's eye fills with a terrain that feels hauntingly familiar, and I am instantly there, somewhere deep in the southwest. Despite my current familiarity, limited to books and movies, the surroundings seem well-defined and distinct. Intuitively, I know this picturesque backdrop paints a past-life landscape from soul memory. It's an unmistakable feeling, like visiting a place from childhood with an essence so deeply tattooed it reaches into bone.

As the vision continues, Dimitri and I ride on horseback across scrubby desert panoramas, the kind baked dry by scorching sun. I sit astride a beautiful chestnut mare; her rich auburn coat glistens in the sunlight. His horse is espresso with an ebony mane. Our late 1800s period clothing speaks of humble comfort: Dimitri's smoky topaz trousers and matching vest offer a rich contrast to his starched, white, long-sleeved shirt, while I drift in layers of frills and lace, my flowered dress framed by delicate edges and a bright white petticoat.

We are two settlers of modest but sufficient means, transplanted in the West. We are to be married or newlyweds; I'm not sure which, but there's a sparkle to our relationship that's palpable, the kind that comes with new love or a freshly forged bond.

While enjoying our escapades through what seem like crimson Arizonian bluffs and ravines, the afternoon sun dresses the day in heat that radiates off the surrounding stones in shimmering iridescent ribbons. We're riding fast, and the wind pulls at my cinnamon hair, making flags that lash against my corseted back.

Dimitri and I round a corner, neck-breaking pace, high above a canyon. I can't see the whole of it, just a brief glimpse of the two of us dwarfed by red rock and the feeling of freedom, far above the world below.

Suddenly, my mare loses her footing. There's no recovery, no walls to stop her. I am falling, slow-motion off a steep cliff into the hungry gulf behind me.

Drifting backward through hot, thirsty air, I catch a glimpse of the intense summer sun. It's nearly blinding except for a silhouetted figure – Dimitri, surrounded by dazzling yellow. A halo of penetrating light surrounds his face, a face wearing a distressed mix of panic and shock. My hand stretches toward him, reaching...hoping...a futile yet human attempt to pause time and the inevitable.

Curiously, I feel no fear. Just a sense of peace cradled by the overwhelming feeling of love and connection with him – a union that death cannot conquer.

I found you again, through time and space into eternity. The words press as a deep inner knowing, flooding me with ripples of awareness. I am full and fully in – heart, mind, and soul. No level of me escapes this knowing – a lightning-bolt strike that ignites a profound love, untouched by time.

I've been with you many, many times, Dimitri. Here we are again.

Another place. Another adventure. Here's to what this life holds.[22]

There is a warmth in your presence,
feeling you beside me.

Out of the corner of my eye,
I catch a flash of your form, sitting perfectly still,
lost in meditation.

I bathe in the heat of your skin against my palm,
fingers entwined in a comfortable embrace.

Immersed, hands resting together as one,
I instantly touch into a hidden part of you,
A soul memory,
a long ago but not forgotten flash in time
that begs to come forth,
like a new babe emerging into the world.

A deep connection relived,
a bond of eternity through eternity,
pulling within my center.

A love forged by distant ties and still present.

It radiates out as light, blinding light,
a new dawn on the morning horizon.

---

[22] **Note:** When I met Dimitri in 2008, he had an intense fear, with no rational basis, of suddenly losing his spouse through a tragic death. My vision gave context to his feelings and our time together offered a way to put them to rest. Even though our paths have diverged, laughter, love, and growth have filled our journey. For that, I am truly grateful.

And in that moment,
I know we have come together, yet again,
to dance a dance on hallowed ground.

Whatever that dance comes to be is meant to be,
and I lovingly accept the adventure
to live this out with you, again, old friend.

Reflections

❖ *What connections have you experienced that feel intense, instant, or oddly familiar?*

❖ *Have you considered these to be connected to past-life memories?*

❖ *How have these connections affected you and why?*

Angels All Around

For he will command his angels concerning you
to guard you in all your ways:
~ Psalms 91:11.
King James Bible

It is He Who calls down blessing on you.
as do His angels. to bring you out of
the darkness into the light.
~ 33:43 Qur'an

Faithfully and lovingly, we are guided, protected, taught, encouraged, and nurtured, moment by moment, day by day. Our Divine helpers love us deeply and remain ever-present, spreading their love from birth to our final transition, as we grow during our time across the veil, and in all the spaces between. Each Helper, imbued with a specific purpose, supports, inspires, and advises us in their unique ways. These include assistance with life's more difficult tasks – loving reassurance when we feel down, guidance in seeing the Truth of any situation no matter how it looks, support to grow – as well as aid with the simplest of jobs or activities.

Our Divine helpers include an array of entities: passed-over loved ones, spirit guides, and angels. Loved ones who have crossed into the realm of spirit provide their assistance to let us know of life beyond our perception of death, to urge our release of misunderstandings and misguided beliefs, and to help move us forward on our path. Their consciousness and evolvement influence all they offer us. In other words, the personal belief system each carries into the afterlife, from their most recent incarnation, combined with what they learn after physical death, determines the help they give. Paying attention to their personality and level of awareness, as we knew them when "living" (in the flesh), often informs the kind of help they provide from the spirit realm.

Guides are entities who previously incarnated on the earth plane. We draw them to us, depending on our energy, which changes as we grow. In other words, we attract our guides based on the path we travel and where our consciousness and evolvement lie; so, their consciousness is reflective of ours. Because of our guides' earthly experiences, they understand our undertakings here and may be better suited to our present lessons as we engage in a purely earth-based life. For example, should we need assistance finding a parking space, we would ask a guide of parking. For help with writing, we would attract a guide knowledgeable in essay creation or journalism according to the task. Often our guides (and we have many throughout our lifetime) are a previous incarnation of ourselves – a past-life aspect with understanding and knowledge of our lessons.

Angels are different than guides. Broadly speaking, they are individualized vibrations of pure Divine Energy, who never forget or become misaligned with Source. The more common angel sightings, witnessing a human-like, winged figure, merely come from our desire to see them in an acceptable form. Many angels solely exist in higher realms, beyond personal contact with humans and other life forms. There, they direct the energies of Divine Essence, serving as the perfect memory of the Universe and all within it; others tend to the very livingness of universes within universes, holding the energy of life with the utmost devotion. In contrast to guides, angels *never* live out an earthly existence. They can, however, occupy animal or human form for a short period to carry out particular tasks or duties to help people on their journey, typically in emergencies.

Every living creation – humans, animals, plants, and the mineral world – has angels to watch over them. We rest in the company of hundreds of thousands of angels. As humans we *each* have 443,000 angels; at least a hundred or more are with us at any given time, and two guard us while we sleep. Our personal angels assist us with small, daily tasks, like choosing our clothes for work or applying make-up. Similarly, our guardian angels offer protection and guidance throughout our day, like safeguarding us while driving or traveling. Some angels, known as devas or earth spirits, also protect and care for our animals, minerals, and plants. Others, yet, inspire our spiritual evolvement and help us learn or teach. There are literally angels for *every aspect* of our life. They bring us little songs, whisper in our ears, urge us lovingly to grow, help us understand lessons and new information, hold the vibrations of healing and love, and remind us of the Truth of our very being. Everything they do, without exception, is for our highest good and *never* against our own will. One thing they *cannot do for us* is to release our limiting beliefs or errors in perception. That, my friends, is up to us!

By all appearances, I've witnessed and communicated more with angels of other people than with my own. Many times, however, my constant chit-chat, snippets of confirmation and visitations, along with remembering their undying devotion keeps angels foremost in my mind.

That said, two highly memorable experiences with my angels – more unforgettable, perhaps, because of longer interactions – merit sharing. The first, an angelic alarm, woke me just before a call from the crisis team while on the night shift.

As the story goes, immersed in a strange and cryptic dreamscape, an image of a television character called Brock, appeared repeatedly. In the back of my mind, I could hear a directive: "Remember the word, Rothrock."

As the dream ended, a beautiful female angel appeared, standing by my bed. With my eyes still closed, I saw her as a luminous white figure with an outstretched hand that tried to wake me.

"It's time. Get up, now," she said, not in words but more as thoughts.

"I'm tired. I don't want to go," I whined, a perfect four-year-old voice in my head.

"You signed up for this," she said, softly but firmly.

Suddenly, my dream ended, shattered by the annoying, adrenaline-dumping, Crisis line ringtone. As it screamed into the darkness, I woke with a jolt and rolled over just far enough to poke the talk button.

"Hey..." I croaked in a tired, raspy voice.

"Hi, Adriene. It's Crisis. I have a client for you."

"Can you give me a sec to grab a pen and paper?"

"Sure. Take your time."

Grabbing the writing supplies left on my nightstand for such occasions, I shuffle into the nearby master bathroom and flip on the light.

"Okay. Shoot. I'm ready."

"Great! The name is Brindle Rothrock..."

As the operator continued to fill in the details of my 2:00 a.m. client, it didn't take long for a strange Deja-vu to fill the air, calling me to review details of the dream just before my angelic alarm.

I must be delirious, I thought, mentally recanting the names my glowing harbinger gave me.

Brock.

Rothrock.

Brindle Rothrock.[23]

Those angels!

---

[23] **Note:** Any connection to a Brindle Rothrock, somewhere in the world, is purely coincidental. This name was chosen for symbolic reasons, only.

Another memorable angelic encounter came as guidance before a devastating car accident in my 20s. I feel very fortunate to look back and witness those angelic whisperings. At the time, I misunderstood and took them as idle mental chatter. How I wish I had listened...

It's a rainy workday, early in the morning but not too early. Dawn has already passed, and rush hour is in full swing. The ride to the hospital where I work is nearly forty-five minutes with moderate traffic, and so a departure shortly before 8:00 a.m. affords me a little time to spare.

Climbing into the small blue Honda CRX, one I share with my boyfriend, I throw my army-green messenger bag on the empty front passenger seat. The rain-speckled windshield warns me that this ride will be longer; it always is on these kinds of days, when wet roadways annoyingly make the miles drag on.

The foggy rear window's hazy view signals a need for caution. So, I slowly back out of my space to leave the ordered lines and macadamed compartments that make up our townhouse parking lot, then lazily drive to the main street.

Pulling out of the complex, I travel down dark, wet blacktop roadway, the first light blinking in the distance. Its red beacon appears fractured by the droplets on my windshield – scattered bits of color that dance between the wiper's clean swipes.

Put on your seatbelt. A thought from seemingly nowhere breaks into my consciousness as I roll toward the light. The taillights in front of me issue their own reminders, telling me to pay attention and stay alert to hurrying motorists rushing to unknown destinations.

There's no easy route into the city coming from Blue Bell. All but side roads and small highways rest between me and the major arteries, as the borders of Philadelphia proper approach. From here on in, it's one light after another with varying lengths of roadway between them, the kind of driving I love – *not.*

As I continue on the double lane edging closer to the city, another light approaches several car lengths away. *Put your seatbelt on.* The thought presses again, and I think in response, *Next light.*

I never wear a seatbelt; I guess it's because I wasn't taught how important they are, but as an adult that's not the greatest reason. They're not legally mandatory (1990) or routine for me, so I can't understand where this thought is coming from. It's strange.

The same exchange happens repeatedly, a regular dia- logue, seemingly, between two "parts" of myself: one that seeks to assist and protect, and the other that stubbornly delays, for no apparent reason. There is one distinct quality to the assist-and-protect thought – it enters my mind in a voice like my own thinking brain. The thing is…it *enters.* It isn't the active churning of mental energy, or the problem-solving part of me, or even the self-talk part of me, like the one that answers it. It's unique and feels more like it was given to me than generated by gray matter. Again…strange.

Driving at an average, steady pace in moderate traffic, I can see another light ahead. It's solidly green, and I look up one last time, yards away from the intersection, as the banter of mental tennis – "me" and the "other voice" – fades into the background. As I approach the light, a white streak takes up my whole field of vision and...

I open my eyes. On some level I'm aware that something's missing – a gap between the white streak and this motion-lessness, my car ominously still. Worse yet, I cannot breathe; the air has mysteriously left my lungs. So, I sit, bewildered...one...two...three...four...five seconds.

Finally, the invisible monster releases its grasp, and I can take a deep inhale. Cool, damp air rushes into bronchioles frozen in time, freeing me from the longest five seconds of my life.

I don't have a clue where I am, and the world seems curiously suspended outside time while my brain slogs through evidence. All I know is that the shattered glass on the front seat looks so pretty. Reaching over to sift through it, my hand dreamily scoops the glossy chunks and then casually lets them fall back into the passenger seat like grains of sand escaping an hourglass. The wind-shield in front of me has shattered: a chunk of bloody hair planted like strawberry-blonde grass sits on the fractured surface, precariously out of place in its new landscape. Strangely, I feel no pain and continue to survey the inside of my bizarre surroundings – a feeble attempt to understand what's happening.

Looking up, the reflection staring back in the rearview mirror sends a shock wave through my dazed body – a gash on my chin threatens to expose teeth that hide behind a veil of blood. The length and depth of the laceration try to push through the murky confusion of my consciousness.

A tap at my driver's side window causes me to slowly shift attention. I am a fly in molasses. Only part of me can process that help has arrived, as a female police officer speaks to me, asking about what happened. The exchange releases a wash of emotions.

Explaining my single memory, "I was going through a green light, then all I saw was a white blur."

In a long pause, I sit and observe, trying to piece together the splintered bits. Nothing makes sense, except this: there is an accident scene, and the central player is me. So I watch, quite out-of-body, as people hurry around my car, like ants swarming to collect their injured sibling. We all wait for the ambulance and rescue vehicles because it's clear that I'm stuck, pinned behind a collapsed dashboard that holds my two knees, sharp plastic talons grabbing flesh; with broken pieces digging into tissue, there's no room to move, let alone leave my vehicle.

Finally, the rescue personnel talk to me about the window, explaining their plan to avoid using the jaws of life. Their words seem garbled and slow, pantomime underwater. Thankfully, they pry the driver-side window out of the way. Because I'm conscious and responsive, pulling me out of the accordion wreckage is simpler.

Foggy from shock and head trauma, everything feels surreal as I'm plucked from my vehicle like a pickle from a jar. Then, surveying the highway filled with bystanders, stalled traffic, and more rescue personal, I see it; silently parked in this sea of controlled chaos is the source of my mysterious white blur: a large white moving van. In one swift, rain-soaked, out-of-control turn, it crossed all lanes of traffic to land directly in my path. The explosive broad-side impact launched its passenger out his window, but he doesn't have a scratch, nor does the driver.

There's an air of shame surrounding them. Neither look at me.

Long story short, my car was totaled – a hunk of crushed metal – so much so that my step-dad cried when he saw it at the police impound. The accident landed me three days in ICU with a suspected cardiac contusion. Thankfully, that wasn't the case, but I did suffer from whiplash, a double concussion, a five-inch facial laceration, a temporomandibular joint contusion with permanent damage, knee lacerations, patellar bruises, and, of course, post-traumatic stress.

After weeks of rehab and time to heal, I know that I am one lucky chick. Had I listened to that voice in my head, which I now know as my guardian angel, my physical injuries would have been negligible. Despite stubborn resistance to those warnings, I was divinely protected and lovingly held.

I am, to this day, eternally grateful for the miracles that happened – escaping death, the impetus to start graduate school, and an appreciation for life – all the learning and growing from one crazy ride.

And of course, a heartfelt thank you to my guardian, for your love, your light, and for your precious angel whispers.

To all the light beings in my life, Namaste[24].

---

[24] **Namaste** – A Sanskrit interjection that means the God in me bows to the God in you.

❖

Reflections

❖ *What are your beliefs about angels, especially guardian angels?*

❖ *Have you ever been aware of angelic help or interventions?*

❖ *What miracles, big and small, can you witness in your life?*

❖ *How have they affected you and why?*

The Door Shade

When your problems seem incessant.
Just be more incandescent.
~ Shaiman & Wittman
Mary Poppins Returns

Man's greatness lies in his power of thought.
Blaise Pascal

A faint yellow glow catches my attention as I reach the top of the stairs. Hurrying to stop our constantly spinning electric meter as it assaults my squeaky tight budget, I trot to the end of our quiet upstairs hallway. Stretching the upper half of my body around the edge of the bathroom doorway, I sneak a quick peek in the mirror just above the small white sink. *Ugh!* Hurled like a swearword at the reflection staring back, my reaction undoubtedly identifies a call for more loving acceptance. Instead, I run my hand down the wall and casually flick off the overhead light, leaving any remaining criticism there.

This upstairs walk-through is the last of my remaining tasks, carefully planned mental checks as I anticipate the end of a long chore list before a much-needed respite:

Close windows ☑

Turn off lights ☑

Close back studio door ☐

Go on vacation!!! ☐

I take a deep breath, ready to finish the list. *Finally.* Next in queue is the nearby studio door. It opens to a back room over the garage below, a frequently forgotten space that sits quietly. Sometimes a creative retreat, other times a bedroom, it's tucked in the far corner of our house and only sees sporadic use.

Reaching out to grasp the cold metal doorknob firmly, I pull the white wooden studio barrier toward me and listen to the lock engage as I've done a thousand times before. The door rattles a bit, tugging in response, a warning of an open window on the other side that beacons, "Close me."

It's just a draft playing with the pressure in the room, I tell myself, pausing to find a reason for the wrestling match. It's not unusual to pull this door shut and watch it pop open again, the latch struggling despite its moving parts nesting perfectly together. This is what the clattering seems, at first – a breeze, a pressure gradient, air trying to equalize itself. But the door begins to rattle more violently, wood banging against wood.

I linger, holding onto the bronze knob while anxiety tinges my guts and ruffles any resolve I thought I had. This is *nothing* like its previous resistances; this aggression feels like something else.

"I didn't see an open window," I mumble aloud to no one but myself.

Pausing to sort through cause while the rattling continues, right hand still holding the knob, mind stubbornly locked on logical reasons – the knob begins to twist! It twists in the opposite direction like someone is hiding on the other side playing a game, opening the door from inside the room!

Shocked, I jerk my hand back, playing hot potato with burning brass, molten metal, while confusion sets a brushfire in my brain. *It's only you up here...you... and...what?* My eyes focus hard and watch the door handle continue its rotation...turning...turning...turning.

All hope of sound reasoning leaves me, and I explode with fear, the air sucked right out of my lungs in one violent gasp. My heart beats like a kettle drum, pounding raucously in my ear, threatening to permanently deafen me. It throws itself wildly against bones, trying to jump through my ribcage and escape the confines of its home. I am fossilized wood, cemented into place by terror, but I can't tear my eyes away. They're glued to this slow-moving knob. Staring. Just staring in disbelief.

Suddenly, the door launches into even more belligerent shaking – the loud hammering of wood against wood – violence absorbed by steel hinges. The caged animal tries to pry its way out of prison while the bars hold fast. My heart screams and jumps into my throat, begging to be caught and held. Feeling like a child trapped inside a nightmare, immobilized by fear and confusion, I'm too scared to run and too horrified to stay. Every brain cell just pulled up ranks and left me here, neurons dangerously ossifying under stress. I am nothing but a giant beating heart with granite legs.

Energy! From somewhere deep within me, an unexpected burst of courage, or just enough terror to get me moving, takes the two legs (surprisingly attached to my body) and seizes the moment. They carry me back through the hall and down the steps onto the first floor as the wooden bully screams behind me, echoing throughout the house. If the landscape outside could reassure me with sunlight instead of its threats to turn inky-black, my legs may have carried me right out the front door, down the street, and into the next town. Somehow, though, the approaching dusk feels just as frightening as the darkness upstairs.

In my front foyer, panting feverishly, I search for answers – in my mind, in my resources – but none surface. So, to quell this nuclear anxiety, I call Jackie. She advises me to pray and mentally fill my home with holy light.

A sincere call for help leaves my lips, an appeal for guidance, but it comes from a place of fear. Of course. It is a prayer, nonetheless.

I retreat to bed. Though I try to rest, fitful flopping is all I can accomplish. The whole house feels overshadowed by nervousness and questions. *Are we safe? Why did this happen? What's in the studio?*

Hopefully, time will answer them all.

Perhaps the best solution is to go on our vacation, to step away from this turmoil and negative energy, I think. Thankfully, the boys and I leave tomorrow. I hope our return brings help, new ideas, and a fresh mindset to make our home feel safe again.

❖

Our week at the beach has helped me gather thoughts and courage. I feel ready to work with whatever energy resides here. Thankfully, support arrived today and I feel more at ease with knowledgeable help. Two spiritual friends guide the cleansing and blessing of our home, offering some insights into what may have happened.

Walking with them, a fearful four-year-old on a ghost tour, I try to understand and sense what they feel. And like a child, I stand behind, always shielded (at least in my mind), as we navigate each room with incense, holy water, and sacred prayer to invoke their cleansing power.

Entering the studio, the shade's[25] lair feels less ominous during the day. Yet, as the sun streams through the window of the room's alcove, I can feel the lingering heaviness, especially around the walk-in closet. It's a vibration I know well but assigned to my imagination. My friends say otherwise, confirming my suspicions, ones that make my hair stand on end.

Walking through the boys' bedrooms, we inspect further as I report on "cold spots" – areas where my eldest's bedroom turned frosty, invaded by nighttime icy blasts – and an odd dizziness that knocks me off-balance in my youngest's closet. My friends again confirm these impressions, the psychic awareness I so want to ignore. They believe a vortex lies under the front of the house, fueling the strange activity and dizziness. Even this seems odd to me, yet, the dogs routinely avoid these rooms, especially

---

[25] **Shade** - an entity from the world of the dead; a ghost.

the closet. I suppose they instinctively sense something – an energy that defies logic.

The house seems lighter after the visit and cleansing, yet I feel like a spiritual toddler – wobbly, conflicted about the world, and in such need of growth. This journey is painful, so I reach upward, which is actually inward. *God, help me!*

Time seems to drag on since my first meeting with the door shade. It's been nearly three weeks and returning home at the end of each day causes dread and uneasiness, especially when alone with the dogs. The boys, at least, provide distractions, their care to focus on. Minus kiddo company, I fight with myself, trying to resist the dips into worry and fear.

Though I rarely enter the studio, merely avoiding it is not enough. It's as if the experience has painted the whole house with foreboding: every room and door suspect. Then come the memories of unsettling energies from years prior. They press on my mind, sometimes igniting even more anxiety of the unseen. *How could I have dismissed these earlier clues – the strange nighttime intrusions, mysterious, bitter-cold drafts, "ghostly" visits with a sense of something negative and heavy?* It's really me, I dismissed, a lack of trust in my faculties.

Fortunately, this acute sensitivity to all energies is slowly making sense. Slowly.

❖

Shifting my internal climate from fear to faith takes dedication and work, a daily practice that grows in my consciousness from seed to sprout to plant. Like all seeds, it began in the dark and eventually shattered its hard shell of housed potential. Now, stretching toward the sun, my consciousness plows through layers of dirty beliefs to cultivate new growth – firm roots that radiate through my days with prayer, meditation, and affirmations. I fill my home with holy light and burn sage to cleanse the space. Two bibles lie open for support, bringing the vibration of written scripture. A crucifix graces our front door, a gift from Jackie.

To keep Divine protection in the forefront, I decide to make another addition: crucifix pendants for both children and myself to symbolize the undying, unconditional love of Christ – a power all entities must yield to.[26] Wearing it lends a sense of calm and a reminder that I, indeed, have more help than what I first thought, the kind that soothes, comforts, and guides the way.

❖

A palpable change is afoot. What has been mere weeks seems like hours, yet our home feels more comfortable and not so daunting when I return at the end of the day, alone. I wonder optimistically, if perhaps the storm is over, hoping in my most enthusiastic mind while continuing to grow in faith. This leap – to practice what I am learning, and integrate it – is one of my most valuable

[26] Rev. Penny Donovan, *Christ Becoming: The Lives of Jesus & His Path to the Christ*, (Albany, NY: Sacred Garden Fellowship, 2018), pp. 235-239.

gifts, an opportunity to grow from mental awareness to heartfelt knowing.

Shifting from belief to knowing, really knowing, is a process. It requires me to be open and allow, to embrace divine protection and sacred nurturing – recurring lessons across multiple lives.

At times, the integration and knowing stay at the forefront of my mind. When they don't…chaos. This must be the definition of hell. So, I continue to pray, meditate, cleanse, and fill the house with light – practices necessary for living here, within these four walls, but also for life.

In the back of my mind, as a misty awareness, there is but one pressing question: *Is this just the calm in the center of the storm? Is it lulling me into thinking all is well?* I hope not. So, my work building faith continues, and I ardently pray that this focus is enough; however, I know full well that lessons often happen in layers.

It's been at least a month since the door shade first appeared. The bible still sits on my bedside stand keeping vigil, watching the night rise and fall as it offers a protective and steadfast presence.

I settle in for a night of peaceful rest. The boys are away for the weekend, making the house more quiet than usual, but the animals keep me company. The dogs, already asleep quietly on the right half of my bed, rest against one another to make a neat row with my legs.

One minute I'm dreaming, the next wide awake. It's nearing 2:00 a.m., and out of nowhere, a low, threatening growl just launched me from a deep sleep, as our smallest dog, Zannah, sounds the alarm, first. Whether it's her volume or merely the sheer shock of her growl that jolted me awake, one thing is clear: my nerves are hyper-sensitive and stuck in their own vigil. In a millisecond, memories of the door bring past to present, adding to this nighttime intrusion and freezing my blood.

Shhhhh! I think to my heart. It's beating just loud enough to give away my position. Thrashing fearfully against ribs that strain to contain it, it sends shock waves through the mattress that feels like a child on a trampoline.

My eyes, wide and cautious, scan the blackness for sha-dows, shapes, or some explanation of Zannah's outburst.

I'd rather have a burglar, I think, shushing brain cells that search for solutions. *At least I could call 911 or fight back.*

More fear thoughts frantically search for ways to escape while scanning for signs of a physical intruder, but only the familiar squares of furniture stare back. Nothing else. Nothing visible, that is. And Zannah agrees in a low, continuous growl.

The room feels thick, stagnant with an electric weight. *Something evil this way comes.* The weight lingers all too closely.

Zannah pauses, making me wonder if her warning to the netherworld is over. I silently pray that she goes back to sleep and falls into the quiet peace that started this evening's rest. Instead, she stands, escalating the level of alarm. From the corner of my eye, I watch her slink around the edge of our bed; she's a lynx. Her face points toward the floor, locked on something below – yes, lower than the bed but still too close for comfort. The threaten-ing rumble from her throat persists in long unending snarls, an angry honey badger that pauses only to catch her breath.

Suddenly, Ash joins her in a chorus of baritone warnings. The two stalk the bed perimeter, drawing a line between this world and the next.

God, please teleport me somewhere else. Anywhere but here! But there's nowhere to go. I'm as still as a corpse, silently praying...praying and barely breathing, a baby chick hiding in the tall grass to desperately avoid the drooling fox.

Silent words trip through my mind, earnestly talking to the Father as I watch my heart and Adam's apple play bedfellows. Thankfully, the dogs and I are home alone and yet, not so. No children, no friends, and definitely no thieves to blame this one on.

A clear, singular thought becomes a goal: *avoid more deliveries from the low astral plane.* I don't like the door shade's new form of entertainment. Even though by all appearances, "it" is winning, I refuse to be deterred.

Nearly seven weeks have passed since the door shade made its first appearance. I've been praying, cleansing, and studying daily. Faithfully.

This morning I entered the garage to take the garbage curbside, a humdrum Friday ritual. The air is pungently heavy with a mysterious acidic odor that nearly knocks me over. But that isn't all. Approaching our tall grey can, a full trash bag precariously rests on the broad, square lid. Covering the inky-black plastic – maggots, hundreds of them! *Strange, we've never had maggots in all the years we've been here.*

Pausing to survey the scene with mixed curiosity, I watch the creepy white worms blanket the trash bag like little, gross squirming polka dots. They drape over their new playground and threaten to spill onto the floor.

Tears begin to surface from the stench like cutting a strong onion. It's overpowering, now, and not from the garbage but from an iridescent veneer of cat urine coating the trash bag, as if to say, "I've got this covered." Literally.

Pausing, I don't have to wonder long to identify the peeing culprit. I've seen him sitting in the backyard for days. My new friend, whom I now affectionately call Michael (short for Archangel Michael), is a beautiful, jet-black cat. He mysteriously appeared earlier this week, sitting in the garden with a protective air about him.

Could he be the one to help dissipate the last of the negative energy?

Despite the ridiculous lore that black cats are demonic or bad luck (so much so that Pope Gregory IX had over 900 of them executed), animal symbolism says...

The black cat spirit suggests that we focus more on our personal power and how we use it. These animals show us new ways of looking at the world and encourage psychic development and intuition.

Power. Intuition. New perceptions. Indeed. This message confirms the past months' events and offers reassurance to see me through. Validation from my psychic friends that Michael, my new enigmatic fur-angel, is here to help, accompanies a sense of protection.

Curiously, other findings in the garage also signal closure. Believe it or not, it's in the symbolism of maggots:

breaking down old, negative beliefs and transforming them into fertile soil for new growth.

Who would have guessed that cat urine and maggots could herald the completion of this wild adventure or any for that matter? Certainly not me. Yet, this second confirmation mirrors my work – dissolving the layers of mistrust and replacing them with newfound faith and power. I cultivated this faith and from it, an internal strength to help me face the door shade, which I banished never to return. Abiding gratitude now fills the space where fear once reigned.

The door shade – not a spirit entity or a ghost but a humanly-manufactured, potent thought-form[27] – came to life via our family's tumultuous dynamics and the resulting emotional charge. Like a proverbial three-year-old, we all participated in the construction of "a monster under the bed" (or behind the door).

My experiential training with this "shade" from the lower astral planes has been invaluable, especially witnessing the potency of thoughts and understanding the import-

---

[27] **Thought-form** – originating from the concept of a Tibetan "tulpa," is energy that can operate as ghost-like manifestations; they are created from thoughts and fed through feelings and emotions. Low vibrational reactions, like worry, anger, and fear, mold thought energy accordingly, as do all emotions and feelings. The more emotional energy, the more "solid" the thought; the more negative we feel, the lower the vibration, and thus the expression of the form and how it behaves.

ance of expelling my inner demons. And, now, being aware of the creations and energies in my life, intentionally conscious of what I feed on an ongoing basis, I can bring forth manifestations for my highest good (fingers crossed).

As for the cold spots, nightly intrusions, and ghostly visits of years past...who knows for sure. Perhaps a vortex or portal was to blame, increasing the visits of spirit entities. Maybe an Indian burial ground or long-ago events, connected to the ancient village that once stood nearby, influenced these other mysteries. At the very least, they offered more practice for my awakening faculties, gifts from the unseen with opportunities to grow in trust.

Thankfully, Spirit always aids us with whatever we create or open to our life, helping us transform it into a valuable lesson. I know I did. Beautifully. Most of all, I came to trust myself and Source. Surrendering control – the little self yielding to the true power of the Divine within – I now possess a new awareness and deeper sense of Self as guided, supported, and loved...all the way Home.

❖

Reflections

❖ *Have you had any encounters with strange energy, thought-forms, or ghosts?*

❖ *How has this experience affected you? Changed your life?*

❖ *What beliefs, operating under the surface of your consciousness, create/feed events in your life like the thought-forms of my door shade?*

❖ *How might you change your mind or shed old beliefs that continue to impact your daily life and influence you in ways that don't serve your highest good?*

Mr. Frog's Wild Ride

Throughout this journey of life, we meet many people along the way. Each one has a purpose in our life. No one we meet is ever a coincidence.

~ Mimi Novic

I f we pay attention to all that happens in our world, we will be pleasantly surprised and intimately affected by occurrences and events, especially those that appear fateful or coincidental. In my experience, there's no such thing as fate or coincidence. In other words, serendipity and synchronicity exist to teach us about the perfect timing and magic of the Universe – to offer valuable lessons and put our questioning about the nature of life to rest. These beautiful mystical sisters demonstrate how the Universe converges to give us exactly what we consciously and unconsciously desire (manifesting in action), as well as what we need to grow (spiritual evolution in action). And though coincidental happenings can vary greatly, sometimes the simplest symbolism appears serendipitously to demonstrate our innate power. Perhaps it even causes us to pay attention to everything occurring in our world, externally as well as internally.

Synchronicity and serendipity may even teach us about our value or show us how much we are loved. At other times, they herald the arrival of a push (sometimes a shove) to use all the tools we have learned, to put into practice in the "worst of circumstances" what we know to ground the experience deep within our soul.

Always and eternally, Universal Power and our Divine helpers bolster us through love and urge us forward; as such, when we pay attention, we also find supportive and reassuring events. Sometimes what happens is so surreal that we can't help but stop dead in our tracks to look, listen, and heed.

One such personal experience, demonstrating the many faces of serendipity and synchronicity, happened amid my tumultuous divorce.

It's the recession of 2008 and I join the masses in a financial wrestling match. Drowning in fear, I feel alone – a single parent with no extended family support. The combination of multiple part-time jobs and a lack of child support make bill paying a challenge. So, I struggle to financially support two young boys and myself and battle gut-punching pain, a sign of threatened survival and primal terror.

While one aspect of the experience I recognize as karmic, my perception exacerbates everything. And even though I am dedicatedly engaged on a spiritual path, I still hold the attitude of lack. Worry combined with current circumstances reinforces my negative mindset, which in turn creates more of the same. It's a cycle that I feel stuck on like a violent carnival ride with no off button.

On the other side of the coin beam two bright, imaginative, caring children, many loving and supportive friends, a rich spiritual practice, just enough food on the table, and a comfortable home, to mention a few. But the message that this time of struggle will pass and I/we are okay is eluding me.

With summer in full swing, an enjoyable treasure trove of activity is here, again. Roasting s'mores, walking barefoot, playing backyard games, and catching fire-flies are the favorites. Life still feels intense, though, as lack fueled by fear hangs in the backdrop with energy that's potent and thick.

Trying to put its pressing away for the evening and give myself a break from worry, I make my way to the neighbors to join the kids. Walking out our bowed vinyl screen door, I turn to check that it's closed enough to keep out snooping mosquitos and discover a pleasant surprise – a tiny, mushroom-brown peeper clinging outside the hash-marked steel.

Knowing how the boys and I love these little frogs, I take my new friend across the street. There it becomes an instant hit among the children, and I relish the time, watching them enjoy the peeper, nature, and all that life offers in this moment.

Finally tiring of froggy games, the boys, gently and respectfully, release the peeper into a tangle of grass yards away from where our two families play fireside games.

As night folds into day, the dawn breaks in pink and yellow hues. Like any morning, I climb into the master bath's frosted-glass enclosure, steaming and heated to perfection.

Standing in the water to wake up while the hot droplets soak my tired body and messy hair, I hope to stay here until my skin is sufficiently pruned. Unfortunately, time won't permit such luxury, so I lazily reach for the shampoo. As my dripping fingers scan the colored plastic bottles, a tiny light-brown blob, clinging just below the silver shower caddy, catches my attention. Squinting through misty air and wet lashes, I see the blob staring back – an angular face, round brown eyes, four spindly legs with tiny suction-cup pads, and a tan body wearing dark brown stripes – a spring peeper! It clings precariously to the frosted glass, a frog identical to the one I found last night on the screen door! *But we released that one across the street?!* I think – confused, intrigued, and totally mystified. Still, the creature sharing my shampoo is undeniably the same.

Obviously, I didn't get the message from froggy's first visit last night; the second…impossible to ignore. Serendipity and synchronicity have, once again, converged, creating a snap to attention.

With curiosity peaked, I take to my resources for the deeper meaning and uncover potent messages from Ted Andrews, summarized into the following:

The spiritual meaning/totem animal symbolism of the frog appears in many traditions around the globe.

This animal, generally associated with the water element and its attributes, symbolizes cleansing, renewal, rebirth, fertility, abundance, transformation, metamorphosis, life mysteries, and ancient wisdom. If we want more abundance and success in our life, frog tells us to change our personal vibration.

When animals make an appearance, especially in such a manner, life offers a powerful message. Any more obvious and I might have found my friend straddling a pile of scrambled eggs! This shower-hopping frog demonstrated just the lesson that I knew in my head but had escaped my heart.

I feel blessed, again. The Universe's reassurance caused me to examine current struggles and remember lessons that I needed to completely integrate. This guidance – to move beyond the limitation of lack and fully trust in Divine abundance – helped me release projected fear by changing old perceptions. The message affirmed a period of cleansing and rebirth into transformation through the ancient Divine wisdom of Universal order – a coincidental treasure in the shape of *Pseudacris crucifer*, or Mr. Mushroom-Brown Peeper.

Now, I see synchronicity as a potent reminder that demonstrates where Spirit is leading me, urging me to grow. Whether my discovery appears "good" or "bad," it's always my choice to find the sweet serendipity and the beauty of the lesson it holds.[28]

Reflections

- *Has serendipity and/or synchronicity visited you?*

- *Can you identify the messages offered?*

- *How could you use Animal Medicine to clarify what lessons you may be working on or help you navigate a challenging situation?*

---

[28] Revised from Adriene Nicastro, *The Soul-Discovery Journalbook: An Intimate Journey into Self, Volume III,* (Pathways to Freedom Press: Bellefonte, PA: Pathways to Freedom Press, 2021), p. 301.

Hide and Seek

The Universe is the game of the self,
which plays hide and seek forever and ever.
~Alan Watts

The cool weight of metal presses against my bare skin as I pause in a moment of reflection and look out the front window. My silvery reminder, an ornate crucifix pendant, has offered a sense of calm and protection in the past months of turmoil and uncertainty, dealing with the door shade.

With fingertips lingering at the hollow of my neck, I allow profound gratitude to replace reflection. Holding the pendant with purpose, I scan the delicate detail – the body of Yeshua suspended on a cross with a garden of tiny flowers beneath his crisscrossed feet. It reminds me of his journey and the symbolism of eternal life, the crucifixion of error perception to end all suffering. Knowing this miniature Garden of Gethsemane lies unmatched to the life-sized one more than 2000 years ago, it still stands as a metaphor that we all have gardens that breed fear and doubt. How thankful I am to have these reminders when I feel pulled from my center.

Excitement breaks my quiet contemplation. I am eager to leave. A weekend retreat awaits, a little over an hour away, and so my pregnant pause shifts to packing.

Three outfits, pajamas, toiletries, a notebook, *this should do it.* I stuff everything quickly into overnight bags and place the two stocked parcels outside my front door. Funny, how they decorate the weather-worn front step that's chipped from years of shoveling and seem to patiently wait for my departure.

One last jaunt through the house will seal the transition from home to an uplifting, insightful weekend. I breathe deeply, feeling the cool air rush through my nose; it fills me with reminders of what's to come…respite, learning, reflection, and inner peace.

Certain that the house is finally in order, I walk out the door and lock it. As I turn and reach down, hands gently stretched toward the brown leather handles of my bags, something feels curiously amiss – an absence of that comforting weight around my neck.

I fumble for the cross (the only cross I wear with fierce regularity), but my hand finds an empty chain. No cross. No Garden. Frantically patting my collarbone and all around the gentle dip there, I search. Fingers explore the entire length of silver, hoping that it's hiding on my back or in the folds of my t-shirt; all but bare links remain. Neither shirt, pants, nor bra caught the escapee. Crucifix…gone.

Now my heart sinks, along with my stomach. Like the pain of losing a good friend, a gut-crushing sucker punch starts to erase any hope for peace. Instead, a growing anxiety creeps in to replace the missing metallic coolness.

This medallion served as a companion, a "source of safety," a harbinger of protection, a donor of light. I feel more alone than ever, an emptiness that pulls at my insides, but I also feel a little silly for the importance I have placed in my silvery comrade. Still, the comfort and help it offered through some very rough patches with our home assigned it such status.

I need to find it! A silent war cry marks an earnest search mission. A bloodhound, hot on the trail of the missing, I look room to room, stripping sofas and chairs, combing floors, pockets, the dirty clothes bin, and countertops. Moving outside, every square inch of sidewalk, front lawn, and driveway meets with scrutinizing visual sweeps.

Nothing. A lonely thought taps the glass of my singular task, and I pause to catch my breath.

It's time to switch gears, trying to redirect myself. *The retreat won't wait. Put away the worry and stress and give it up to a higher power.*

"Alright, angels," I request aloud. "Please bring my crucifix back to me. If I'm still meant to have it, that is. If, however, someone truly needs it more, I bless it and release it to them."

With one last hopeful look across the lush green landscape, my eyes reflect a deep desire – the longing to see sunlight orbs of a mirrored surface flash in return: Morse code for "I'm here!" Instead, another silent prayer floats from my lips into the ethers: *Bring it home. Please.* Mildly reluctant, I climb into my car and slowly back out the macadam driveway into the weekend.

❖

The retreat delivers plenty of time to reflect on the loss of the crucifix. A friend suggests that perhaps the experience is an opportunity to internalize what I still see as being supplied from outside of me.

It's true that not long ago I needed it to feel safe, to remember that I was protected, that the Christ, Source, the Universe had my back. *Do I still believe that comes from outside of me?*

I guess so. Look at the fear...my desperate search. *Didn't I already embrace the spiritual symbolism of the crucifix, the Living Christ, the unconditional love of Source, as part of my very being?* Evidently, I'm still looking outside.

Through the weekend, affirmations flow in and out of my consciousness.

I am safe.

I am protected.

God is within me.

I am love – the love of Source, a Child of God evident in the Christ of me.

How could I be separate from Source?

I can't.

In my own mind and heart, I begin to feel a new presence of Home.

◈

With the weekend ending, I use the ride back to "normal" to help me transition, to ground an awareness and feeling of Divine care and safety. Gratitude grows for the experience, for the shadow self it exposed. I accept that my crucifix may live elsewhere, perhaps even with a new person, a someone else to help.

Driving down the highway, the blur of trees keeps my lower mind peacefully busy while the rest of me integrates all that has come to pass.

Feeling the usual whole-body drowsiness from a weekend filled with rewarding spiritual work, I slowly return to the world, a strange transition, always.

The welcome sight of my house brings a sigh of relief. As I pull into the driveway, the summer grass glows a warm shamrock-green in the evening sunshine. Before turning the key, I sit quietly in the car as the engine hums. The reality of home and the week to come slowly filters into my awareness, while I look for the resolve to move.

Finally, mustering the energy, I grab the silvery door handle to release the lock and lean on my car's beige armrest. The door seems heavier under tired muscles, but a firm push helps it swing wide over the charcoal macadam. Pivoting my tired body to exit the vehicle, I place a foot on the ground, as I've done a million times before. But in these pedestrian and automatic motions, the ordinary suddenly shifts to extraordinary, when a silver sparkle catches my eye! At the top edge of my pink converse sneaker, the rich detail of the lost crucifix stares back at me. Unable to move, I freeze under its mesmerizing spell.

Immediately, the attack mode of rational linear thinking tries to flood neurons; they feverishly fire, seeking answers to the questions that hungrily grab at my consciousness. *Where? How? Caught in my tire?*

Nope! I have too much faith at this juncture to allow confusion or doubt get a firm grip. *Move back, logic! There's not a molecule of reason to handle this one!*

Goosebumps accompany a smile that rises from deep within me and registers on my lips.

Those Angels...Thank you!

Reflections

❖ *Have you ever lost something valuable only to find it in an unusual way?*

❖ *Ever consider that angelic help or passed love ones may be intervening?*

❖ *What might they be trying to communicate? A lesson? A gift? Both?*

The Trickster

The true shaman, the true naturalist,
works to reconnect conscious human life
with Nature and Spirit through totems and ritual.
- Ted Andrews

Spirit never fails to offer pleasant surprises and doses of wisdom, especially when we least expect it. Receiving these messages always depends on our willingness to be open and listen.

As we become centered, vibrationally up, and tuned in, the gates of heaven open wide within us, a gilded glow of truth to light our way. Picture a tree - arms to the sky, willing to receive while firmly rooted - able to take in spiritual energy from above and earth's sustenance from below and use them.

To follow spirit guidance requires focus, dedication, and movement beyond the earth plane's illusion and glamour. Then we can witness life's true purpose - learning vital lessons, those required to navigate our world and evolve.

Our lessons, which often seem like the acquisition of knowledge, are really the *unlearning* of old patterns of being. Unlearning always requires releasing blockages or perceived limitations held in our thinking and emotional patterns.

Surprisingly, personal messes, difficulty, crisis, and chaos are beautiful lessons in disguise. On a moment-by-moment, day-by-day basis, paying attention to *all that presents itself* – events, happenings, and symbols – can show us our Spirit's call, the pokes to examine our life. In fact, what appears to lie outside ourselves offers valuable clues to understanding what's inside, adding context to our internal climate and active beliefs. This is the meaning of "As within, so without."[29]

For me, some of the most impactful and potent opportunities for growth arrive through spiritual retreats. Here, the group intentionally welcomes Divine helpers, who infuse the event with a healing climate and higher vibration. Richly flavored with the impetus for movement and development, retreat opportunities present themselves as ripe fruit on the vine – the kind ready for harvest – especially when participants use introspection and release the limiting beliefs and old patterns that no longer serve them.

Additionally, these kinds of gatherings have an overarching theme, one chosen beforehand by the facilitators (but influenced and impressed upon them by Spirit), one that draws a particular vibration of help from the other

---

[29] "As within, so without" is a Hermetic principle based on spiritual law that says what we hold in our beliefs about ourselves and our world manifests outside of us as events, situations, relationship dynamics, etc., tricking us into thinking that life happens *to* us instead of *through* us.

side. Shaped by the group's needs, themes evolve from general to specific, support collective and individual intentions, and influence discussion and experiential exercises. Because themes guide interventions undertaken – the straightforward ones and those that meanderingly or covertly surface – they help members unravel the mysteries in their lives, sometimes in the most unusual ways.

All spiritual retreats hold surprises, transformational shifts unique to each person present, even the facilitators. One such weekend event, with a colleague of mine, I remember well.

Our group has gathered on a lovely spot of land peacefully nestled mountainside. Dense woods line the property like decorative lace, giving other-worldly fringe to a manicured expanse of grass that hosts a beautiful stone abode. The dewy, bejeweled lawn – set ablaze by the morning sun – glows electric green, highlighting pink, yellow, and blue flowers in full bloom.

The retreat gatherings – split between the outside near the property's waterfall and the adorable garage studio apartment – make this time feel blessed and magical long before we begin. Between the mountain, the stream, the waterfall, the gardens, and the woods, this feels like paradise.

Standing at the apartment's back patio, my colleague Asher and I wait patiently for our last participant to arrive. That's when I see him.

Peering through the tall grasses just over Asher's shoulder is a coyote. His angular snout points in my direction. Intense coal-colored eyes and coarse tannish hair distinguish him from the surrounding weedy-green strands. Shaded by a narrow leafy canopy, he watches carefully, as if waiting for something only he knows.

Shocked, I freeze.

Coyote and I stare at one another from a distance, eyes locked. Time holds us in suspended animation, and the pregnant pause makes the whole world fall away. He feels much too close for comfort, though it's only my unease that's apparent.

Breaking focus, I turn ever so slowly to look at Asher, searching for a way to explain our visitor and my concern. Avoiding an alarmist approach, I hesitate, probing through reason and possible courses of action, but my words keep trailing off.

"Umm...I think...There's a...." Sentences disintegrate into thin air.

My eyes furtively glace back, visually retracing the path to our clever friend. Now, the tangle of mottled sage and avocado grass lies empty, surprisingly unaffected by one full-grown animal.

"I saw a coyote directly behind you, Asher! It scared the crap out of me! But when I looked again, he was gone!" Asher and I laugh, mostly at our unusual guest and the strange beginning to the weekend.

For the time being, I shake off the sudden upset to re-center. Using a moment to get my bearings, clarity strikes from somewhere beyond: Wile E. Coyote isn't from here.

His journey to the retreat site wasn't a path through the forest because he's not in the flesh; he's an other-worldly visitor, a spirit animal (one that I saw objectively, not in my mind but appearing to my naked eye).

Shaking my head with an air of humor, I walk indoors with Asher to officially start our weekend event, out of the furry trickster's influence. A question, however, continues to press on my mind: *Why was a spirit coyote here?* It lingers in the background like a mysterious fog.

Perhaps, time will tell.

❖

The retreat moves quickly into introspective endeavors, diving deeply within the blockages and thought patterns that continued to disrupt our growth. These habits create the twists and turns in life – the thought-emotion-behavior loops that keep us stuck in unhealthy relationships, poor self-care practices, personal sabotage, and more. So, to make much-needed changes, we explore the gardens of our minds, which require a bit of weeding (or a lot!). Like loving gardeners, we gently and diligently look to the devil's thorns of our erroneous thinking, remove them by the roots, and replace the problematic pests with new mindsets befitting psycho-spiritually-minded folk.

Anyone who's attended an introspective retreat knows the work is *not* for the fainthearted. These gatherings, while challenging, reward those brave enough to cleanse their soul – a proverbial carwash for our eternal memory. To further our progress, we welcome assistance from the spirit world's higher vibrations, calling in angels, guides, Master Teachers, Source, and our Higher Selves. Yes, we need all the help we can get. And, fortunately, we get it – support, encouragement, prodding, and guidance.

One unique and special note: The position from which we enter these weekends is insignificant. The labels of leader, teacher, student, and participant all bleed into a workable and grace-filled amalgam. Whether we lead or join as a group member, transformation and healing happen. Sometimes we teach. Sometimes we learn. And everyone heals in the beautiful wholeness of giving and receiving.

Now, back to our furry friend. Wiley's appearance stealthfully begins to move from mystery to magical as the theme of our retreat comes into greater clarity. We explore, watching ego in action – using intention and surrender mixed with humor and lightheartedness instead of negativity and harsh self-judgments – and move past its influence. And what do you know? This theme perfectly aligns with the messages of coyote, the little trickster who nearly fooled me:

Coyote makes you laugh, even painfully at lessons about yourself. Coyote's own trickery fools him. He falls into his own trap and yet manages to survive. Even after bruises and bangs by the experience he goes onto greater error forgetting his mistakes. In the folly of his acts, we see our own foolishness. Self-sabotage refined to sheer perfection. He takes himself so seriously that he can't see the obvious; for example, the steam roller that is about to run him over. That's why when it hits him, he can't believe it. "Was that really a steamroller? I better go look" and he is run over once more.

The cosmic joke is on ourselves and everyone if they follow coyote medicine. Coyote is you, me, booby traps, jet airplanes with toilets that don't work, blind dates, and all the humorous and whimsical things we encounter along the way.

To employ Coyote medicine, look under the shallow exterior of what's happening and why, to clearly witness your own self-sabotage. Find humor in life, laugh at your own mistakes and goof-ups, and be playful when faced with another person's difficult behavior.[30]

Coyote was a gift, a harbinger to heed. He reminded me how ego – the vibration of fear that always opposes Source – stands on the path Home yelling, "You can't!" "You're not smart enough!" "You're not worthy!" Ego manipulates and threatens to keep us under its dominion – a motive that opposes our spirituality and thus spiritual growth – until we learn to *make it our servant*, not the other way around.[31]

---

[30] J. Sams & D. Carson, Medicine Card: The Discovery of Power Through the Ways of Animals, (Santa Fe, NM: Bear & Company, 1951).

[31] "…another approach to the ego, one that explores the concept from a spiritual context. In this framework, our ego is seen as an aspect of who we think or believe we are – the little self that includes the rule-bound, the gratification-motivated, critical, immature, hyper-responsible, emotional, and shrewd aspects all rolled into one. While the distinction between our commonplace understanding and the spiritual may seem relatively thin, the difference lies in what appears as a mere opinion or attitude versus who we think we are in totality – the very vision of the little self that attempts to separate us from our Divinity." Adriene Nicastro, *The Soul-Discovery Journalbook: An Intimate Journey into Self, Volume III,* (Bellefonte, PA: Pathways to Freedom Press, 2021), p. 144.

Now, coyote has a special place in my heart. Thank you, you furry little devil, the omen of ego and all its foibles, criticisms, traps, and talents! I promise to see this wild ride called life with new eyes – to saddle up with joy, a sense of adventure, gentle discernment for others' projected challenges, and humor at my own humanness.

❖

Reflections

❖ *Do you notice any habits, emotional patterns, or behaviors that interfere with your personal evolution? What might you do to change them?*

❖ *How might Animal Medicine help you on your journey of self-discovery and in life?*

❖ *How does ego try to sabotage you and your endeavors?*

The Bridge

I believe that imagination is stronger than knowledge.
That myth is more potent than history.
That dreams are more powerful than facts.
That hope always triumphs over experience.
That laughter is the only cure for grief.
And I believe that love is stronger than death.
~ Robert Fulghum

The light from the alarm clock blares like a small beacon across my bedroom, a space dressed in bluish-black hues. It's just before 2:00 a.m., not a time anyone needs to be awake except medical personnel, burglars, and parents feeding tiny babies. Anyone, that is, except for me.

I lie here entirely, annoyingly awake – eyes wide open staring into the night, like a hoot owl. This is my third evening (technically morning) of wakefulness in a row, and I'm starting to believe that the forces-that-be have assigned me to some mysterious vigil. "Keep the night company," they say.

A heavy silence permeates my surroundings. It's broken only by a loud, spontaneous exhale from the dogs.

Thoughts of meditation cross my mind, a way to give rest to weary bones when the brain refuses to sleep. So, I sluggishly hoist my tired body to a sitting position while the headboard's rigid wooden slats provide a stark reminder that I am, indeed, awake. Settling quickly to keep sleeping dogs quiet, I tuck the blankets around my waist to prevent a chill from sneaking into the warm space between me and the cool early-morning air.

A deep breath clears the thoughts that wind their way through my brain – tiny chattering birds clamoring for attention. One by one I drop the awareness of my physical form...the bed...the room...

Without warning, an invasive energy – hauntingly familiar, like my mother's chaotic aura – lands on me. As the vibration creeps over my skin, its heavy veil attempts to inhibit breathing, being, or movement. Though unsettling at first, I intentionally move beyond it, leaving its oppressive assault at the door where it attempted to enter and continue into the Void.

Passing into Silence, a vastness where time is non-existent and universes collide, I find peace. My peace. It echoes in the darkness, filtering unconsciously from places seemingly forgotten but never lost. Adrift in an ocean of black, points of light swirl in cosmic pools. I rest there, embraced by a familiar and distinct feeling that lies well beyond words.

On the earth plane, minutes pass into an hour, until the awareness of my body, headboard, and bedroom enter again. The weight of being "here" brings mixed feelings as I return to my typical corporeal existence, trying to stay with the peace that accompanied me from the Void. At least, dreamland calls – sleep announcing its arrival for a second time. Finally.

Sliding deeper under the covers between slumbering beasts, I allow my head to merge with the soft curves of my pillow. There I meet the restful otherworld somewhere amid starless darkness and dreams with semicohesive storylines. They float aimlessly – smoky tendrils of past and future, drifting metaphors that momentarily pass by, then dissolve. Nothing gained, or so it seems.

The sun presses its warm honey light through the distant trees, calling my eyes to open and greet the day. But an earlier alarm lingers in a foggy memory – an unexpected phone-song near 4:30 a.m. trying to force its way into the space between new sleep and first light. I met its desperate chime with skepticism, leaving it to echo alone in the silence, while the rest of my consciousness lived far away from any earthly concerns.

Serious emergencies and death. These are the only reasons for such harsh wake-ups, I tell myself, trying to quell any anxiety about what I missed. *If there was something I could do, someone to see, another call would have followed on its heels.*

But nothing. Not at 4:30…not at dawn…at least not yet.

It's nearing nine, and a new call breaks the cheer of a single bird singing outside my bedroom window. I don't know for certain but somehow suspect it is a death call and the answer to my strange pre-dawn alert.

As the phone's chime hangs in the air like slow, heavy raindrops, my mind drifts to earlier. *Who calls at such an hour?*

The pull to greet my harbinger snaps me back to attention. Glimpsing at the handset's ID, I know that the infrequency of this caller (my one and only sibling) is a sign of seriousness.

"Hello?"

"Hey," he answers with an air of intentional restraint, followed by a long pause. "I wanted you to know that dad passed in the middle of the night."

Silence now fills the space as I collect my thoughts: my vigil, our past conflict, his long illness. Like seemingly mismatched puzzle pieces that suddenly begin to fit, gray matter connects all the mysteriously unrelated. Honestly, I'm not altogether surprised – by my newly forming puzzle or his death.

"When?"

"Around 3:00 a.m."

"What happened?" I ask while connections simultaneously continue to form, points of light across all time and space linked by luminescent threads. My early morning vigil seems to be more than a coincidence.

"He had a heart attack."

"When did that happen?"

"Around 2:00 in the morning," he replies flatly, clearly upset but attempting to keep it to himself.

My 2:00 a.m. awakening. Dad's 2:00 a.m. heart attack. My 3:00 a.m. vigil closing. His 3:00 a.m. passing. Events stamped by synchronicity. Should I be surprised? Still, questions flash in front of me again: *Who calls at such an hour? Who calls at such an hour when rescues and visits long deemed impossible slip through fingers as time and fate do our bidding?*

Possibilities fall away, and the answer to my question peeks out from behind a mysterious cloud.

Grief.

Shock.

Disillusionment.

That's who calls in the wee hours when the world lies fast asleep, dreaming of far-off adventures or fighting demons in the darkness.

Caught in a vortex of emotion, people reach out, alerting us even when there's nothing to be done. No rescues. No visits. Just silence. The sound of one hand clapping. Lost relationships swallowed by unsettling quiet.

Then again, perhaps it's the dead calling out to those they left behind? Are they crying into the void between this world and the next to make their eternity known?

"You still there?"

"Yeah, sorry. Just thinking. He certainly lived longer than the doctors gave him."

"Over two years," he adds.

"But this isn't what they diagnosed. I mean, he died of a heart attack. That's not what they said would kill him when they gave him three months to live?"

"No. No, it's not."

"You alright?"

"Yeah. I'm okay. I just hope he didn't suffer."

"Me, too."

"Mom was with him the whole time."

"Ummmmmm...that's good," attempting to cloak my mixed feelings about her presence, though it did inform what I sensed during my meditations in the wee hours before dawn – invasive, heavy chaos malignantly blended with clingy energy.

Time passes quickly in this crazy place. It's now been three weeks or so, but I've been grieving this loss much longer than that. Sometimes, I miss him, but often I don't know what I miss. He was a man I didn't know well. Perhaps, it's meant to be that way, or perhaps I knew him better than I realize? Maybe he wasn't so complicated after all? Probably, just probably, I miss what I think I could have had. Isn't that sometimes the case?

Another weekend retreat serendipitously falls on the heels of dad's passing. Here, clarity, peace, and support can fill the space left behind by loss.

"I see a man in spirit," she says, a reading from my be-loved teacher and weekend facilitator Penny Donovan. She sits across from me explaining the message, her ghostly-white hair shining under the bright overhead lights.

"He's standing on a bridge waving at you. He looks like he's trying to cross, and you're telling him that it's okay to go. *'Go ahead,'* you tell him. He looks a bit sad, but as you encourage him, he crosses and waves goodbye from the other side."

Gratitude and calm wash over me. This is the final piece. Funny how our seeking poignantly finds resolution.

"Thank you for the message. Yes, I had to make peace with him, to let go so he could decide to go Home. Spirit woke me for three nights at the same time. I believe that I was with him, helping him prepare."

"Yes, you helped him pass," she said, reassuring me.

And so, it goes…I wasn't awake to keep the night company. I was keeping dad company. And mom, too.

How ironic, our contracts and agreements. Crucial hours intuitively offered to a man I spent nearly my whole life with but barely knew. We connected through the ethers, across timelessness in a sacred space of healing.

Interestingly, my step-father's transition came a few short weeks after I had said goodbye in my mind and heart, a farewell to a relationship resting on mysteriously thin veneer. Our connection lacked a depth and honesty that had become too painful to bear – the crush of inauthenticity contaminated by his refusal to acknowledge my mother's abuse or accept his role in it. All that remained laid in fractured pieces – the result of his precarious clinging to denial. In his final years, he repetitively recounted news accounts and similar ramblings that mirrored my early childhood family dynamics, conversations too hypocritical and confusing for me to actively carry forward. I guess I'll never know his intentions or the reasons behind his maddening stories. Perhaps he secretly tried to say that he disagreed or felt remorse? Then again, maybe he was just perpetuating the denial that began so long ago. All that transpired between us – the protection I hoped he would offer as a rational interceder – called for more forgiveness, forgiveness removed from the face-to-face connection with a man unable to do the work.

Now, I know that he did the best he could. It's all we can ever do.

So, I chose to leave our sporadic and infrequent visits in the company of other fond memories and cherish the short time the Universe gave us to reconnect after his terminal diagnosis in 2007.

The Bridge pays tribute to the gift of my step-father's transition, one that I feel honored to have taken part in, one that added to my understanding of life beyond death and the eternalness of love no matter how messy it gets.

Thanks, Dad. I look forward to seeing you, whenever you decide to visit, knowing that you're just a thought…a heartbeat…a dream away.

Until we meet again.

❖

Reflections

❖ *How has the passing of a loved one touched your life?*

❖ *Have you received signs that they're with you?*

❖ *What unresolved conflict or relationship challenges still linger with this person?*

❖ *How has their passing helped you embrace the gift of their relationship and all you received/gave as part of that connection?*

❖ *Is life's messiness and all that's transpired in yours giving you more opportunities for compassion and understanding? For forgiveness of human fallibility and personal sticking points?*

Seven Vultures on a Roof

Life is one big road with lots of signs.
So, when you riding through the ruts,
don't complicate your mind.
Flee from hate, mischief, and jealousy.
Don't bury your thoughts, put your vision to reality.
Wake Up and Live!

— Bob Marley

I don't usually ask for signs, especially to help me make decisions or plans. Typically, inner guidance - the whispers of where, how, and when to go this way or that - tends to be enough to move me forward in a particular direction. Other times, it's just a pull or tug, like feeling connected to an invisible towline.

The most challenging part of following inner guidance or intuition involves belief and trust. In other words, knowing that I'm receiving information clearly - absent some attack of fantastical imagination - is a process, and not without hiccups. Regardless, I always intend to live in tune with Spirit, and as a result, life has offered many lessons to help move me out of my own way, like one memorable occasion when I asked for a sign.

The event in question was The Weepies concert. The band members just happened to be childhood friends of my then-partner Dimitri. Because the group was playing in Philadelphia, making a trip to my old stomping grounds was an outing we both looked forward to, especially Dimitri, who hadn't seen them in years.

Excited to meet Dimitri's friends, we planned our trip, a short overnight jaunt on a summer day much like any other. The day before, however, a pending sense of doom washed over me, a gut feeling that we should stay home and abandon our plans. These intuitive hits left me quite baffled. I guess I'm more comfortable with "yes" directions than "no" ones. Moreover, I didn't trust myself, and as a result...controlled chaos.

Repetitive thoughts swirled, clinging to my insides. Mulling over what sticks like dried glue, I wonder, *Why am I feeling like this?*

I'm normally so excited and optimistic about road trips and mini-outings. But something feels off, I think, trying to shake the unsettling feeling that pressed on my consciousness.

Typically, Dimitri is the worrier. He frequently expresses concern about a litany of things going wrong, especially when trips approach. As a result, he makes plans and backup plans, lining them in neat rows well in advance. Not me.

Trying to ignore my internal climate, I go the closet, pulling out a bit of this and that – dressier mixed with comfortable – along with a bag to hold my wares. I plop my armful on the bed.

Folding the clothing into tidy squares, I attempt to stack my thoughts and feelings into a neat pile as well. They don't comply as politely, though, and squeeze neurons besieged with information too unsettling to overlook.

Unable to contain my angst behind more silence, I blurt out, "Something bugs me about this trip!"

"I don't feel great about it, either!?" Dimitri's voice holds an air of confusion and surprise, a confession that trails off into the nearby closet he faces.

"But that's typical for you."

"I know, and that's what I thought. Just me worrying," he explains. "But it isn't typical for you?"

"I know. Too, strange."

We consciously put our conversation and concerns to rest for the night and ask for a clear sign to signal what's for our highest and best regarding tomorrow's adventure.

Sweet dreams...

The following morning, the same cautioning energy remains. What I discover on my way to early morning wash doesn't help. A small basement flood covers the laundry room and spills into the adjoining game room, leaving a sloppy mess.

Stomping through the swamp, I lay out every clean towel sitting on the dresser that holds linens awaiting a trip to the closet. All I can do is attempt to stop the ongoing spread into the adjacent rooms.

"Diiiiimmmitriii!" My voice breaks the peace of our early morning as I yell up to the kitchen.

"Whaaaaaatttttt?" His anxious response, clearly, took a cue from my tone. How he hates cross-floor communication. Shouting just adds to his concern.

"Something's leaking...." My loud words trail off as I search for a way to gently deliver the news. But his rapid, heavy footsteps – a sign of nervous approach – interrupt my announcement and echo throughout the basement,

"What the...." Dimitri sighs with a shudder, surveying the mess.

It didn't take a rocket scientist to see that we now live amidst a newly formed bog. The only particulars missing are frogs, cattails, and lily pads.

"I think something around the furnace is leaking," offering a clue to the disaster.

Dimitri and I briefly investigate the problem further. Indeed, something near the furnace overflowed. Now, the questions press on both of us: Can we find a repairman and will he fix the problem before we need to leave for the concert?

Rushing upstairs to reach help is the easiest of our next steps. Waiting is the hardest. By first reports, though, all seems in perfect order. A repairman, now on his way, signals positive movement, but as the clock continues to tick, time appears to fight against us.

The morning drags on…and on. The repairman, delayed.

I feel drawn to ask for specific guidance…but differently. Retreating to my meditation space, I hope clarity prevails.

Quieting the chatter of gossiping brain cells, a message finally filters in: *Better to stay home, but know that regardless of your decision, you'll be safe and protected.*

The words are clear, but my mind wants to fight them. Something still seems off, and I feel split. Like halves that can't reconcile, parts of me argue, jealous siblings vying for attention.

Maybe I just don't like the answer, especially the push to stay home?

We should cancel.

Buzzkill. Party pooper.

Come on! What could be problematic about a short trip?

The critical me shames. The rational side seeks reason, concrete thinking that tries to intercede. But doubt's hulking shoulders begin to crowd out any trust in myself, in my ability to get the information; there's no room for both. Clearly, I cannot simply accept the guidance.

Two painfully long hours after our first conversation with the tool-box-wielding savior, we return to the basement to do as much cleanup as possible. Nervous creatures trying to erase evidence of a problem, we wait and mop. Wait and dry. Wait and scrub.

"Maybe this is a sign? First the leak, now the repair guy is really late," I complain, stomping around our shrinking marshland. "I *still* feel funny about going and then there's the message in meditation."

"I'm sure it's nothing. It could be ego trying to sabotage us. Let's not have this spoil our fun." Dimitri encourages me to stay positive and stick to our plan. Clearly, he sees this more as an obstacle to overcome than a sign to abort our mission.

"I need to pick up the boys from the pool," I announce, walking toward the steps. "I hope he's working by the time I'm back and that it doesn't take too long," calling loud enough to let my words trip down the stairs, while I make my way up to the front door.

Off into town I go, gathering the swimmers – our two boys and their friend – to retrieve them from the university natatorium. After dropping our carpool addition in the more distant suburbs, the return drive home brings us to Meek's Lane – a winding, narrow back road behind our neighborhood that cuts through the woods. The boys banter and my mind wanders, mulling over our trip, broken furnace, and basement swamp.

Suddenly, coming down a hill, just before a sharp turn, I catch a glimpse of something strange – mysteriously massive shapes roosting high on a house. I ease off the gas to get a better look, and the car rolls forward ever so slowly as I take in the bizarre sight.

What are those enormous Halloween decorations doing up this time of year? I wonder, staring curiously at several statuesque, dark-winged creatures along the roofline.

Then, unexpectedly, one of them moves!

"Oh my God! Look, you guys!" I shout to the boys and point. "On the roof! Up there!"

One, two, three, four, five, six, seven...turkey vultures perched on the sharp ridges of a housetop. Tangled wings – small parked airplanes, drying from this morning's deluge – extend ominously, feathered appendages that cast gargantuan shadows, as the creatures jockey for position on the narrow roofline. Frightening and foreboding, the sight of these birds sends chills up my spine that register on the back of my neck. Hairs on end. Weighing on the breaks, I can only stare at their black-winged bodies as they swallow every inch of space and turn a perfectly adorable abode into some living, breathing diorama. An All-Hallows' Eve horror show.

"Don't stop, Mom! They're too creepy!" My oldest pleads while slouching down in the back seat, hiding from the monsters. His brother points, mesmerized by the scene.

Too creepy for even a teenager to appreciate, these giant shadowy fowls look like harbingers of death. The image sears gray matter, burning dark outlines into my mental mindscape – threatening silhouettes contrasted against a cloudy sky. *I wonder if the owners know what kind of "creepy" they are sporting?*

Returning to the safety of our birdless home, we tell Dimitri about our adventure, one so surreal. Even more ridiculous, the serviceman continues to work on a problem reported as minor, despite repair that began over an hour ago during my departure.

Hmmm....

So, we busy ourselves with chores and wait. Finally, after three hours our furnace repair is complete, but it makes getting to our concert seem even more impossible now.

I must pause here to offer a bit of retrospective consideration. It's beyond me why we are sticking to our plans. The flood, the late repairman, the vultures, and the prolonged furnace fix should be enough to signal a stop. But no. We're stubborn. Moreover, we refuse to accept signs offered by the Universe. Convinced some ego challenge lies at our feet, we see obstacles to surpass instead of warnings to avoid difficulty.

Lessons are afoot.

The results of our perpetually delayed morning bleed into afternoon, and we venture out for the concert, hours past our set departure time. It is, though, just enough to reach our destination.

Driving along, summer showers surround us in thick waves, alternating with dry spells marked by perpetually threatening skies. Furthermore, the Universe continues to issue updates along our rain-soaked journey, mental visions of flash flooding. They poke through my consciousness as we travel on riverside roadways near Amity Hall toward Harrisburg, the half-way point of our trip. Shown to me as heavy, rapid rainfall that assaults highways and overfills streams to block traffic, these mind's-eye images suggest a warning that I share with Dimitri.

We continue, however, pushing past our concerns, trying to deny any significance in them.

Stopping for a travel break in Harrisburg, we talk to a waiter during lunch.

"Where are you headed?" He asks with concern that registers on his face.

"Philly...for a concert."

"Just be careful. We've had some serious flash flooding. Roads nearby are closed."

Dimitri and I look at each other. *Seriously?*

Yup...flash flooding. But what do we do? Continue, of course. The message, "Better to stay home," echoes in my mind, massaging brain cells a bit too gently. You see, Spirit doesn't press with volume. It quietly speaks in the spaces between, never shouting or competing with the voice of ego. As such, the guidance comes in ever so softly, which doesn't help me trust what I'm feeling. (Guess I'm looking for a brick to the head.) Thankfully, all along the journey, spiritual tools help me stay centered and keep the white light of protection around us, a constant for me. At least, I employ these.

Finally, we arrive in the suburbs of Philadelphia and prepare to shift from the turnpike to the city's infrastructure. Approaching an exit to get on the Schuylkill expressway, a main artery into the city, Dimitri's face displays a mix of mild distress and frustration as our online mapping program is set ablaze.

"Look at this!" He growls, holding up his phone.

Red lines pollute the screen. Like manic chicken scratch, they indicate numerous bottlenecks. Now, even Google screams, "GO HOME!"

With traffic at a standstill, we float in a stagnant sea of honking metal boxes, all traveling in the same direction but seemingly frozen before the next visible exit. It's the kind of inching forward that can tax even the toughest nerves, and I feel the clock eating away, tick by tick, at the short distance between this moment and our concert's start.

"This is crazy! Let's take the back roads!" I announce, breaking the tense silence between us.

Knowing the area, I hope that local side streets will provide an anticipated escape from the chaos, so we roll ever so slowly toward the exit ahead, Gulf Mills – a residential area bordering Route 76. Inching along like snails (who definitely move faster), finally, the stagnant energy parts, and we take the exit.

Patting ourselves on the back with an air of pride, a smug smile on our lips, only brief moments pass before our bubble bursts; cars stack less than 100 yards on our new route, and we sit bumper to bumper. Again. So much for progress! But that's not all. A state of disbelief replaces any lingering frustration and foolish arrogance, accompanied by a sense of awe, shock, and "I told you so."

We sit in the wake of sheer destruction. Ancient, stately Sycamore trees stand twisted in half like twigs; plants and garbage lie alongside lawn furniture, randomly scattered by something other than human. This and litter pepper the properties lining our path, accompanying the lifeless neighborhood power lines. As we creep down the narrow roadway, bewildered residents, agitated and dazed, fill the streets like ants recovering from a callous home-wrecking boot.

I put down my window, seeking clarity. "What happened?" I ask, catching one passerby on the street.

"A tornado!"

"When?"

"Not more than five minutes ago!"

"I'm going to check on a neighbor," she says with urgency, trying not to abruptly brush us off.

Yes. A rain-soaked tornado touched down a short five minutes before our arrival, taking trees, furniture, and whatever else it could grab along with it. This, in Philadelphia, no less. Uh-huh.

Now, I know you must be thinking: How many signs do you need, woman? Clearly, too many to claim we possess some semblance of intelligence. This time, though, we take in the message. Finally. A little slow...or a lot slow. I know.

Searching out a driveway to reverse our direction, we backtrack to our hotel for the night and forfeit the concert, less than thirty minutes in the future. Even in the best of circumstances, we can't make it. Under these circumstances – impossible. The fact that I'm even commenting on the math...ridiculous.

Dimitri searches for a local radio station to fill in the gaps – details about weather and the trail it left behind. We catch a few news briefings: a semi-truck, lifted into flight by the tornado and hurled across a mall parking lot into nearby buildings, now sits lifeless, a large metallic heap.

Trees, local power, and structures are either bent or broken under Mother Nature's wrath.

A feeling of gratitude, safe passage, and Divine protection blooms. Awareness sinks in.

I think to myself about all the warnings we chose to bulldoze past, signs left unheeded – a feeling, a damaged furnace pipe, a basement flood, a direct message from Spirit, a late repairman, seven vultures on a roof, an uber-long repair job, a late departure, flash floods and flash-flood visions, standstill traffic, and a tornado. Slow, stubborn...perhaps even stupid, and yet we remained ever wrapped in God's loving arms, just as my message said.

Arriving home, adventure behind us, the long list of signs weighs on my mind. So, I take to spiritual material, considering all that transpired. First, I witness how the basement flood symbolically matched the storms and local flooding en route, the chaos which ultimately ended our trip. Had I heeded them earlier in alignment with my intuitive feelings of caution, a sense that we should change our plans, we could have avoided much stress. Still, all our delays synchronistically provided the perfect interruption to keep us from the tornado's path. The most fascinating sign, the one burned in my memory – the birds. *Ted Andrews here I come...*

> The vulture teaches us the cycle of life, death, and rebirth, helping us to see the process at work within our lives, and its appearance is always a signal to trust in that process. Regardless of how events and

situations may appear, the vulture reminds us it will ultimately work out to our own health and benefit, helping us to see more clearly how events are likely to unfold. The vulture helps us trust in what we are sensing around us. They help us see or at least sense the cycle of change as it comes upon us so we can work with it.

Priceless! The vultures alone offer a snapshot of our entire adventure. They reinforce the message that all things work for our highest and best, everyone safe and sound. The storm's destructive energy demonstrated new beginnings, a dissolution of the old, and life's cycles in action. The lessons in trust, especially in my own intuition, remain – a lovely tattoo on my soul.

So, here's to being in the flow, in the Tao. Certainty emanates as we step into this Sacred River, the Clear Stream within each of us. Next time, though, I'll trust my senses on the first alert. (Oh, how I hope!) And undoubtedly, I'll keep an eye out for those turkey vultures!

Reflections

- *Have you ever noticed the gut-level pull of intuition or instinct warning you about something? What about prophetic dreams or visions?*

- *What did you do? Listen to them? Ignore them? Question them?*

- *How might you be more attentive to your internal guidance or employ it for help?*

Responsibility's Weight

Man is condemned to be free:
because once thrown into the world.
he is responsible for everything he does.
~ Jean-Paul Sartre

Responsibility. Duty. Culpability. These are the echoes from childhood...from lifetimes. The feeling sat squarely on my shoulders, a physical manifestation of burdens and duties born of responsibility's weight.

I wasn't always aware of this heavy sense of obligation. Throughout childhood and teen years, it operated unconsciously like breathing – naturally, innately, and without thought. Stealthfully leaking into my 20s, it caused unintentional consequences as the bad feelings I carried toward myself, internalized from difficult family situations and other relationships.

Functioning as the consummate accountable party – family symptom bearer, whistle-blower, designated driver, emotional baggage carrier, bill payer, etc. – I excelled at being responsible on so many levels for this, that, and the other thing. Yes, I held the burdens that arrived in ugly little packages as other people's disowned thoughts, feelings, or actions. In other words, I'd take on how another felt or what they did as my own, believing it was mine to feel, to worry about, or fix. When someone's poor choices or disowned parts came knocking at my door, I opened my arms willingly. Sometimes people tried to forcefully place them on me, but other times I just absorbed them, unaware of what it was in me that made the energy stick.

Unbeknownst to me, I carried out the empath's silent code – take on the world's pain because it's so excruciating to let another suffer. (Rule #1: Empath's Handbook. Kidding...but not kidding.)

Why was it so easy for me, even oddly comfortable, to assume this position? When we're expected to carry things for others, especially parents, we routinely apply the same assumptions/responses to all those we meet. This early programming means that we commonly see ourselves as either the source or the repository of another's feelings, thoughts, and deeds – even if others don't believe this. Moreover, we magnetically draw people that mirror our family of origin to repeat the patterns created through early encounters. [32] Add to this an empathic constitution, a make-up partially created and totally fed by unhealthy and entangled family inter-actions, and... Voila! A toxic cocktail of "all yours, honey; so drink it up."

---

[32] Adriene Nicastro, *The Soul-Discovery Journalbook: An Intimate Journey into Self, Volume III,* (Bellefonte, PA: Pathways to Freedom Press, 2021), pp. 509 -512 & 519-521.

My relationships since childhood bear witness to this theme. For example, when the daughter of a family friend bullied me with a punch in the stomach, I didn't go to any adults because I worried that she would get into trouble. Or when my mom blamed me for her personal feelings, I became riddled with guilt. Accused of making her behave in a certain way, I became angry, while under the fury lay a cesspool of self-blame and shame for causing her pain.

In adulthood, I became less entangled because my internal barometer began to register a "Not Mine" reading. And, by developing stronger boundaries and listening to my gut, I grew in understanding, witnessing the hidden motives behind other people's words and actions. Looking back, I see a slow process; guess that's just the nature of my evolution.

When I first became a healer, a healer of the mind, carrying clients' emotional pain verified a more evolved but certain resurfacing of the same energy. I intellectually knew what wasn't mine, but the old tapes – my pain is your pain, my problem is your problem, my behavior is yours to fix – still lingered enough to expose another layer of personal transformation. In addition, being highly empathic compounded the internal pressure from old family messages and contaminated my understanding of what belonged to me vs. others.

To be an effective therapist and centered person meant that I needed to address the rescuer tendencies linked to unhealthy accountability. So, I focused diligently on shedding the patterns that didn't serve me, a task buoyed by years of observation, reflection, and releasing. Thankfully, dedicated psycho-spiritual self-work offered more context and understanding, as well as the tools to navigate as an empath.

After much self-focus and transformation, I started to feel a sense of completion around hyper-responsibility, but the Universe said otherwise. This is the nature of learning (really unlearning and deprogramming) which arrives in so many shapes and sizes: lessons appear concluded but remain hidden – all coy and stealth-like until they come full circle to seek new completion. This was, by design, my ongoing (and hopefully final...but perhaps not) lesson on responsibility. Maybe I should have expected it to surface again, yet I didn't. But surface again, it did...

It's the early 2000s. I've just been offered a position as a crisis counselor. This opening, a way to help others navigate intense turmoil, sits outside the box of my typical venues of treatment. At first, I hesitate. This is not the work I feel drawn to, but here lies this opportunity. Part of me knows that it comes for a reason, but conflicted about the position, I require a clear answer. Surely, by now, you can guess for me that's a trip to meditation and a journey upward in consciousness, which is actually inward, deeply inward, to Self.

My sacred space, a room for meditation, clients, and energy healing is my go-to. Peaceful and serene, filled with crystals, books, and plants (a mini jungle to be exact), this spot lovingly embraces and sustains while helping connect me with the world in a centered way. Sitting down in my comfortable wicker chair, I set clear intentions to be aware of my Higher Self for Truth, holding the question of the crisis position on a "mental" altar of sorts.

Quieting my busy brain by removing all focus from thoughts, I allow my breathing to slow. Everything passing through my awareness meets with purposeful detachment as I simultaneously let go, releasing the space of my healing room, body sensations, noise outside, and any lingering mental chatter. This process isn't describable by words. Words are too limiting. But I can say this: for me it's like being in the middle of a traffic jam that softly but definitively shifts to standing in a crystal blue mountain lake warmed by the summer sun. This is where I now rest, embraced by and infused with wisdom and love. Joy and peace.

The question held in my heart before entering this space has an answer. "Yes." I know and feel it all at once, but discomfort and doubt flood in behind the information as ego puts on boxing gloves, its attempt to derail guidance. Still, I cannot erase the sense of knowing. So, I accept the position with a strange curiosity as a question forms lightly in subtle tones: *What does Spirit really have in mind?*

What I quickly experience as a crisis counselor surfaces first as intensity, the razor-sharp acidity of people's mental and emotional pain, the kind born of life-or-death emergencies caused by severe internal turmoil. Working with clients who struggle with suicidal and/or homicidal thoughts and feelings, I am face-to-face with the art of true detachment – to help, guide, assess, and problem-solve in a centered way, unhindered by the worry of outcomes that I have no control over. I can only do my best and wait, a process that requires time and patience on my part, time and patience with others and with myself.

My job, without a doubt, has a responsibility that can provoke fear, a mind and heart churning with angst. A perpetual blanket of concern – the potential of having a client pass traumatically – threatens to suffocate me. Anticipation and worry malevolently lurk like a threatening black cloud in the back of my brain. Rationally, I know with the rate of suicide steadily increasing in our population, the number of people in crisis skyrocketing, it's only a matter of time that someone I counsel will successfully suicide.

It's been many months since the start of my new position. Commonly, I return home from work filled with apprehension: *Did I do enough? Did I take the right actions? How long will the person stay safe?*

Questions like these frequently filter through my consciousness, if not actively keeping me awake at night, then woven through dreams. Sometimes the fear runs in the subtext of conversations and activities, like a smokescreen too thin to see but quietly caustic. Thankfully, my spiritual work gives context and support; the support I suspect will increase over time, support I graciously welcome.

The news arrived through the web: a report posted in typical fashion on a locally-produced site. I never check the news except for an occasional jaunt through *The Week*

magazine, but today, Spirit found a way to bring me into the internet's media onslaught. That's when I discover the sad update: a former client's untimely end, crossing over through suicide. For confidentiality's sake, we'll call this person Blue.

Upon my discovery, I immediately connect with Blue to send healing through loving intentions and energetic reaching into the higher realms. As in all cases, physical death doesn't end the possibility of receiving; we continue to take in prayers, energy, love, and healing on this side of the veil and after passing.

During the healing, I psychically see Blue in self-imposed isolation, in emotional and mental pain, like all those who leave the physical plane thinking they will escape their agony through suicide. The angels can't come near to assist because Blue won't let them, mostly out of a feeling of unworthiness. As an empathic imprint, the weight rests squarely on my chest.

Through spiritual education, I know that when a person crosses through suicide, they feel a sense of shock and panic. As the body dies and the silver cord of life becomes severed, the new separation from their physical vehicle registers abruptly with the knowledge that they cannot return to occupy it. As a door, of sorts, closes, the regret of their decisions, impulsive or not, press on their consciousness. Desired escape from all earthly turmoil – a need or desperation that materializes through completed suicide – proves unsuccessful and frequently amplifies their pain because their emotional and mental bodies remain with them.

On the other side of the veil, resting in the astral plane, those passing through suicide also witness the heartache caused to those left behind. Physical separation from family and friends is immediately recognized and further demonstrates an inability to return to the body and a life they left behind. If their self-destructive act comes with a great desire to punish others, they discover the immense price of that punishment: anguish and blame cannot be released just because the body is gone.[33]

With Blue's death, I, too, feel regretful. Responsibility and duty ring their warning bells again. The burden presses its ugly hands at my throat, accompanied by a feeling that says I missed the mark; I didn't excavate Blue out of onerous pain. This sense of failure hounds me, despite any logic. And though I know that Blue remained far outside my influence for many months, the feeling still hovers around me – a heavy storm of dark thoughts and oppressive concerns.

To counter the onslaught, I dive into reflection and enter the peace of communion with Source. From this a vigil emerges, and I, again, do what I know – send healing, love, light, and prayers[34] – focusing on Blue, not me. Soon, I will rally all those who attend an upcoming retreat to do the same.

---

[33] Rev. Penny Donovan, *Suicide.* (Albany, NY: Appleseeds Publishing, 1995).

[34] "…prayer, light, and love, the expressions of our love-light? All are gifts we offer the world through our inherent Divinity – an extension of Source, an expression of our Holy Nature through Union. Spiritually speaking, we are prayer, light, and love, which become known and expressed most especially when we embrace our Self and the raindrop knows it is One with the River." Adriene Nicastro, *The Soul-Discovery Journalbook: An Intimate Journey into Self, Volume III.* (Bellefonte, PA: Pathways to Freedom Press, 2021), pp. 335-341.

❖

It's quite common that unresolved lessons and/or old hurts come to light just before our monthly retreats. So, in that way, one could say this retreat is no different; near the full moon, it aligns with planetary energy, spiritual lessons, and all that's for our highest good, bringing what needs to be transformed to light.

All through the retreat weekend, I feel Blue's presence and begin to clarify the intensity of my discontent – the weight of responsibility I carry for both of us.

I urge Blue to accept help from the Angels of Transition and to "sit with me" in the healing chair to receive.[35] My heartfelt desire is to be a conduit for Blue, to ease discomfort, begin the process of grace-filled acceptance, and help transform what transpired in Blue's life, as well as their abrupt and violent passing.

After the healing, I receive a message from Blue through another psychic, an offer of gratitude for my help, smoothing their transition across the veil. With this comes a sense of peace for Blue and myself.

While I wish I could offer more context to the medium – history, concerns about friends, family, and the things that Blue struggled with – I can't. Confidentiality prohibits it. Still, their story for this lifetime ends with more closure than I anticipated. For me, I think the chapter closes, too – lessons learned and healing given and

---

[35] During spiritual energy healing, we can be a conduit on many levels. One way is to receive the energy and transmit it to the person intended. The person need not be physically present, in a body, or know that the healing is taking place. Like prayers, the energy goes to them (across all time, space, or dimensions) and can be taken in as they are ready to receive it, which could be in seconds or lifetimes.

received. I understand that another's responsibility is not mine to bear, and with it remains a heartfelt acceptance that everyone carries their own weight; that *is* how we learn and grow. Moving forward, I know there will be times when all I can do is offer love, light, and healing. Everyone has their own journey.

As a sense of completion filters into my awareness, the subtle integration weaves its way through levels of being, a closure before driving home and leaving the trans-formational space of the weekend. The challenges and lessons I worked through with Blue feel clear, though I share nothing with retreat members but warm gratitude.

As tradition would have it, the group gathers for a final meal before leaving and launching ourselves into the three-dimensional strangeness that we all know well. Eating heartily, the consequence of spiritual energy work – essential grounding and nourishment for a body – provides a necessary and welcome earthy task.

At a round table dressed in white cloth, I speak with Rev. Penny, our retreat co-facilitator, sharing casual conver-sation while lunch ends.

"Thank you, Penny, it was a beautiful weekend. I discov-ered some powerful lessons around responsibility."

"You're welcome." Then without pause she offers, "You know, you were a Druid during the French Revolution. What I see is a long line of people waiting for execution. You knew you had only a short time before they would all be gone, dying at the guillotine. So, you found a secret stone passageway near the execution site and one-by-one, smuggled person after person to safety, among them, your two children now. You rescued all but a few, but eventually, someone discovered your doings and fatally stabbed you. This is where your deep sense of responsibility comes from, the disappointment that you couldn't rescue them all."

I sit speechless, a pregnant pause to absorb what I've been given.

"Thank you, Penny. That makes so much sense to all I've walked through in the past weeks, especially this weekend. You've really helped tie loose ends together."

A humble nod from this gentle soul brings our exchange to a close and with it, a deep sense of appreciation. I feel full...again.

I am so thankful. My lesson revealed its conclusion: old tethers to a past life. Responsibility...duty...the I-must-help-fix-it-or-people-will-die feeling. It was this sense of impending death that sat so precariously, pressing as a crisis, literally and figuratively. It is, without a doubt, the force behind my responsibility and a potent element of the do-something mindset that's driven me my whole life.

Reignited by a family dynamic written through sacred contracts, I am clearly ready to fully discern what is mine to fix and what isn't. This is what Blue's lesson was all about. The root cause – delivered in words taken right out of my consciousness and offered by Spirit through Penny – presented a vital piece of the whole puzzle. Feeling a sense of profound closure and clarity, one more layer of mistruth dropped away in the shining light. Gratitude, healing, and peace fill a place in my heart.

As for Blue, there's an abiding sense of honor. Thankfulness, too. I pray that Blue is reading these words right now, taking in worthiness and compassion, resting in ever-present Divine help.

I lift you into your highest knowing, Blue, that you heal whatever pain led to your untimely death. Thank you from the depths of my soul – for the lesson, the opportunity to know you, and the gift of your beauty and grace. May you rest in and truly embrace how much you are loved.

Reflections

❧ *What sense of responsibility do you experience regarding yourself and others?*

❧ *Is it healthy and balanced or disproportional and detrimental?*

❧ *How has this chapter influenced your thoughts/ feelings about suicide?*

❧ *Has another's suicide impacted your life? How?*

❧ *How would it feel to send prayers and healing to them after reading this chapter? Even if they passed?*

The Accident

*You realize now that life itself is a channel
and that you are constantly receiving.
~ A Course of Love
D: Day 216*

The summer breeze pushes its warm air into the living room while night rests as a curtain, an indigo ink that outlines trees, plants, and the deck railing.

Kaleb lies contentedly on the living room sofa reading, as I pass in and out from meditation to evening chores, just puttering.

POP!!

The shocking sound of metal on metal or metal to macadam. I'm not sure which, but it grabs my attention with such force that I look at Kaleb, our gaze meeting one another, wide-eyed in concern and surprise.

"What was that?" He asks.

The question, tinged with anxiety, hangs in the air.

I stare at him, searching for answers, our eyes mirroring one another's disquiet.

"I don't know, bud, but it can't be good. Not a gunshot… it sounded like a car…like a car that hit something?"

Investigating, I walk out our sliding glass door onto the deck and toward the noise. Houses and trees melt into the evening blackness. Even our nearby park that lies beyond the street behind us is indistinguishable. It's there that I listen for clues, but only quiet permeates the landscape. Not even traffic on the roadway to my right disturbs the night, let alone evidence of an accident. I can't make out much of anything but silhouettes in the dark.

Dimitri is out looking at the stars that decorate the evening sky. He heard it, too, but wants to dismiss its importance. "Probably, nothing," he says.

I attempt to return to the kitchen, to the leftover dishes and remnants from evening snacks, but I can't. The echoes of the sound press on my mind, so I take to the phone.

"911. What's your emergency?"

"Hi. I don't know for certain, but I heard a loud, suspicious noise in the near distance, facing my rear deck. It seems to have come from the park behind our house. I'm concerned because it sounded like a car crash, but I can't see anything."

"We've had no reports of an accident, ma'am. Where do you live?"

I describe our location and the direction of the sound.

"I'll send some officers out to investigate."

"Thank you. Have a good night."

"Thank you for calling."

Kaleb and I discuss the noise again, our unsettled feelings, and the 911 call. I've done what I can, or so I think. But despite my actions and talk with Kaleb, the pressing won't stop. It's become a palpable urge to go toward the noise, perhaps to help.

"I'm going to the park. I need to go, even though I don't know why," I announce to Kaleb and Dimitri.

"I'll join you," chimes in Dimitri. I truly welcome the company.

I'm dressed for bed in a short cotton nightgown, even though Spirit clearly has something other than sleep in mind. So, I jaunt up our beige-carpeted steps to add sweatpants and a sweatshirt over my existing ensemble. *I'm not winning any fashion shows with this frightening get-up*, I think, hurrying to make my way back downstairs.

Grabbing slip-on sneakers from the hall closet, Dimitri and I head for the door. Silently, I wonder if my messy layers of clothing might cause unintended problems – worry thoughts fueled by a perfectionist brain, a fashion-police script from earlier days. But a bigger part of me doesn't care, as the urge to discover our mystery sound pushes its way into legs ready to move.

I yell down the hall to Kaleb, "We're heading to the park. The police are on their way. I'm sure it's fine, but I feel the need to go. Wanna come?"

"No."

As I re-enter the living room, Kaleb's firmly planted stance attempts to quell a growing angst, his nervous look unveiling empathic senses already overwhelmed. Staying at home is a better option for him.

"No worries. I'll call you if anything important comes up. See you soon," reassuring him with a kiss on the forehead before Dimitri and I head out the door.

We walk quickly down the sidewalk toward the park, the concrete squares meeting our feet. Shoes shush in soft scuffing sounds – sandpaper against wood. I cannot determine if the noise is trying to quiet my sense of urgency or wants to help me build momentum. Regardless, a growing exigence surges in electric potency, pouring into every cell of my body. Its distinct hum pushes and prods. This call from the unseen – a call that compels me forward – begs response, and I know it.

My legs, struggling with our restrained pace, break into a trot, moving with purpose. Dimitri meets the change in speed, a sign of support. Jogging past the park's trees and over the path's gentle rise and fall, visions begin, flashes in my mind's eye. I see Seth, a teenager and old childhood friend of my children. *Seth was in an accident recently – is that why he comes to mind?*

Is my brain braiding events, filling in gaps with the recent past?

What if it is him, though? What if he's been in another accident?

Somehow, whatever waits beyond the park feels intrinsically linked to Seth.

As the path ends at the mouth of the parking lot, Dimitri and I scuff over black gravel to the raised grassy barrier near the paved roadway. Streetlights dimly glow, barely breaking the sky's blue-black intensity. In the distance, however, other brightness beckons; distinct yellow beams cross into a dark, wooded terrain that threatens to swallow everything whole.

As we move closer, the road ahead becomes visible under the aid of police headlights. Golden-white tunnels travel through the dense murkiness, flanking a car that's hardly visible. Two officers stand silhouetted in the sea of light, walking around the scene.

"I think I know who's there, but I'm not sure," explaining to Dimitri as nervousness invades my voice.

My mind, expecting the worst, anticipates sights that eyes and psyche would rather avoid. *That won't help.* So, I tuck the worry into my front pockets and focus on the task at hand – helping in whatever way I am guided.

Finally at the scene, the car in question sits in full view as Dimitri and I pause to survey the damage. Glass diamonds grab all surrounding light: broken shards of window and windshield that dazzle the street with unwelcome decoration. A wheel is missing, lying in the grass. The entire driver's side smashed, as if the vehicle rolled over and lost its shape under force and crushing weight.

No one should have walked out of that car...no one. A shudder chases the thought and runs down my spine.

I walk up the hill to where one officer stands, near a macadam path elevated from street level.

"Can we help?" I call to him as Dimitri follows silently beside me.

"Were you the ones who called this in?"

"Yes, but I didn't know what happened. I just heard the noise and thought it might be an accident."

"You were the first to call, much earlier than the only passerby. We're waiting for the ambulance. Someone's very lucky," he says, gesturing toward the figures to his far left.

"Can we offer some company while they're waiting?

He nods, so I turn my eyes to the shapes higher on the hill.

As we walk up the path, only outlines remain, silhouettes created by bright police headlights. All the forms melt into one another – age, gender, clothing, and colors disappearing as the night and backlighting swallow detail. We come upon the figures and stand above them over the culvert. A person of slight build, barely visible – the victim, I assume – lies on the ground with two others on either side.

A deep desire to help, even to merely offer company, competes with a doubt that says, "Stay back." Approaching the cluster, I feel like an intruder in a private catastrophe. I guess I am. The fact, however, that Kaleb, Dimitri, and I make up seventy-five percent of the witnesses, says otherwise.

Softly calling to the group, "Can I come down and sit with you?"

A vulnerable "Yes" from the darkness washes away some hesitation, enough to allow movement. So, I make my way down the grassy embankment. Dimitri stays well behind me like a nervous shadow. He seems too intimidated by direct interaction and keeps his distance.

Standing by the group, still cautious and respectful, I inquire again, "Can I sit here?"

A nod comes from what I can see, now, as a man on the right side of the accident victim. Taking a seat beside him on the gravel-filled grass, I can feel his worry. As my eyes slowly adjust against the bright police headlights, a teenager comes into focus; he's lying prostrate in the grass, lower half stretching toward the road. His body violently shakes in post-traumatic shock, adrenaline coursing through his veins like a million cups of coffee downed all at once. One shoe is missing, but by all accounts, there's not a mark on him. No cuts. No blood. At least nothing is visible to the naked eye under these shadowy conditions. As I consider the state of the car, this young man's wholeness feels surreal. Unlike I initially thought, he's not our childhood friend Seth. In fact, I've never seen this kiddo before, nor the man next to him, a man I suspect is his father.

"Can I put my hand on your shoulder?"

He nods.

This is good, sighing in relief, reassured that he can, indeed, move.

Gingerly, I place my hand on his shoulder, careful to be tender and slow.

"Is that okay?"

Again, a nod.

"What's your name, buddy?"

"Cameron," he whispers through chattering teeth.

Without hesitation, I send healing energy, the cool ripples running like chills through my core, as I speak to him calmly, reassuringly. "You're doing great, Cameron. What you're feeling is normal, just all the adrenaline running through your system. Breathe with me...slow and deep. Just see the breath enter your body through your nose. Let it out through your mouth and with it all the fear."

I continue to talk, to guide him through meditation, and over time his shaking settles while I speak and send healing. I wonder about his dad and ask if he's okay, too.

"Very grateful...very grateful," he mutters nervously.

"Yes, Cameron's quite lucky. I've been in some bad car accidents, and you're very, very lucky. Those angels are working overtime with you, bud."

At this moment, a person crouching like a small apparition to the left of Cameron comes to my attention. I know that a silent presence can be powerful support, but this youth sits wordless, motionless out of stress, not strength – so much so, they remained nearly unnoticed. Perhaps they escaped my attention in all the chaos, or maybe their statue-like presence is what diverted my focus. Regardless, I'm now intently wondering how they are feeling. It's certainly clear that they care about Cameron. For some reason, though, I feel drawn to get a better idea of who they are and why they're here.

As my eyes try to focus, I struggle, again, against the lights of the police car backlighting faces. The bright beams shine just enough to test my vision, as I concentrate and allow details to align.

A sense of shock and curiosity strikes.

"Chelsea, is that you?"

The young girl nods, and I see what eluded me before. I stare with a mix of warm humor, awe, and gratitude at Seth's younger sister, squatting like a paralyzed animal next to Cameron. Now I know why I needed to be here – to help, send healing, and support not Seth, but his sister and her boyfriend!

"Are you okay, Chelsea?"

She nods, still in shock.

"Cameron's really lucky. He's gonna be just fine," reassuring her, hoping that she can take it in.

We patiently wait as I continue to talk with Cameron to support and help him process his fear. Finally, the ambulance arrives. We all watch the EMTs transfer him onto the gurney and into the back of the ambulance. I know he's where he needs to be – off to the hospital for some tests, checking for any remaining nonvisible injuries.

I wish him good luck as the EMTs begin assessing vitals and then return to those remaining – Chelsea, Cameron's father...and Dimitri, who escaped my attention in the flurry of activity. He speaks with Cameron's father, trying to help him make a peaceful transition to the hospital. As for Chelsea, the nights events have noticeably shaken her. So, I reassure her once more and offer a hug to help soothe her overwhelmed and tearful emotions, a natural reaction to all she witnessed. I know that she'll be fine, too.

As Dimitri and I walk home, I have time to allow what happened to filter in. I feel a mix of quiet reassurance, gratitude for safe passage, and validation for following my inner guidance.

We are all called to only be helpful. Sometimes that means action. Other times it means words. Silence. Support. A mindful ear. Many things help in the right measure, appropriate to the situation. When we follow our intuition – the voice of Source in us – and trust Its counsel, we will know what to do.

I'm so very glad that I did.

Reflections

* *Do you recognize the voice or feeling of intuition?*

* *Do you listen to it, ignore it, or reason it away?*

* *What does it feel like as compared to the fear messages from ego?*

* *Where has it led you?*

* *How would listening to your intuition be helpful?*

The Psychometric Scarf

The only real valuable thing is intuition.
~ Albert Einstein

Like many, I find unusual clothing fun and expressive – a way to allow what's inside to be seen on the outside. However, living in a relatively small town often limits clothing selections and challenges my eclectic displays. But using resourcefulness and the internet, possibilities abound, technological blessings in this age of information.

There are many opportunities to exercise expression through fashion – finding just the right outfit to rock a new look. So, I say treat yourself. But if purchasing something for no reason feels difficult, there's always Christmas, Hannukah, Kwanzaa, Mother's Day, Father's Day, Valentine's Day, anniversaries, and my all-time favorite – Birthday (capitalized and without modifiers because it really should be a holiday, at least with our own families).

For me, gifts of self-care are necessary, though I also love holiday treats – Birthday, the most. During the summer of

2014, my Birthday involved a special dress, one crafted with care – artistically designed and ethically made. Who knew that a simple celebration would bring such an impactful metaphysical surprise? Nonetheless, here's what the Universe delivered: new Birthday clothes wrapped in lessons to further my growth.

Today, a family member wants birthday ideas...or, rather, Birthday ideas. I'd like a tunic of sorts this holiday, asymmetrical and unique, a short dress/long top that's casual enough for daily wear but dressy enough for dinner out.

Taking to the internet, I head to my favorite site for shopping – Etsy. Shopping on Etsy gives me goosebumps. Crafts, art, clothing, jewelry, pottery. There are sooooooo many choices!

Typing in "dress" and "asymmetrical," I discover designs and fabric that tempt every aesthetically-driven bone in my body. Before long, a layered two-piece tunic graces the page, custom-made in textured black patchwork from a small family-run business in China, or so the site explains. A bit skeptical, I read the company "About" section, seeking to avoid slave labor shops.

Reassured that my decision is indeed ethical, I send the order details to my generous gifter and anxiously await its arrival.

Weeks later, a small, tidy package from overseas, wrapped in brown paper, sits on my front door stoop.

Bursting with curiosity, I dig through the crisp tan bundle and uncover my treats. A lovely note from the company lies atop the layers of soft, black fabric, explaining their fair wages, retirement packages, and company atmosphere. Tucked within the tunic's dark folds is a bonus present – one silky grey scarf, peppered with kaleidoscope butterflies.

Grasping the billowy softness, I hold the scarf, facing the sunlight that warms our living room, and examine its refined detail. Its mellifluous charm draws me in, and without a thought I wrap it around my neck, tying a loose knot at the soft dip where my collarbones meet.

The day unfolds, a morning and afternoon of clients blend with writing, reading, and meditation – ordinary and uneventful.

As day turns into night, this busyness meets stars, slumber, and stopovers to the astral plane. There, vivid and unsettling dreams crowd the hours of sleep...

Looking through the soot-stained glass of a tiny barren apartment, I am a young Asian woman who shares space with my elderly mother. We squeeze as comfortably as possible into a closet-like room that's worn and harshly sparse. Our movement feels bound and limited, painfully constrained. This is what we know, sharing meager living quarters that barely meet our basic needs – a bed, a sink, and a toilet, umbrellaed beneath the neon signs of a cityscape. I know, without a doubt, that we live from hand to mouth, our days darkened by hunger that lingers behind meals made of broth.

The image switches to a small factory. Here, my Asian mother and I serve as two out of ten workers. We sew long hours for very, very little pay – slave labor. The conditions are unforgiving; tired bodies push through pain and struggle as hours bleed from early light to dusk. Endless work and rushed production fill the space between.

Sewing machines drone a mind-numbing hum that blankets the factory floor. The air reeks of sweat and fear. This is our existence: scarf after scarf after scarf. The profits are never for us. Forget fair wages.

The depth of sadness and despair fills a well in the pit of my stomach – my sadness, my mother's sadness, the other workers' sadness. It caps an anger, a silent fury fed by injustice.

Unexpectedly, perspectives reverse. I am now myself, seeing the young Asian woman, her mother, and all the workers as an outsider looking in. An intense desire to help, to push them out of their place of resigned comfort, to contemplate a plan, wage a revolution. Feverishly, I hoist myself atop a battered wooden table and plead, "Band together! Stand up for yourselves! Don't let them treat you like slaves!"

I yell at the factory boss, who faces me. My eyes are fiery with indignation. "No more work until we're paid!"

Suddenly, I'm awake, and frustration lingers behind my racing heart. Details of the dream burn holes in my consciousness. Instantly, I know the source of this turmoil, the creative director of my dream – psychic contamination:

Psychometry /sī'kämətrē/ – psychic reading of objects through the energetic imprint of their creators, owners, and history.

The potency of my unwashed scarf weaves tales, its energy dropping into my aura as a detailed psychic stamp. I can still feel the young woman, her mother, and their friends, the taste of sweat and bitter oppression that lingers malignantly on my tongue.

Deep compassion floods all senses as a silent prayer forms on sleepy lips.

Dear Mother-Father God,
Bringer of Light,
Forgive me for unknowingly
contributing to their pain.
Thank you for lifting them into
their highest understanding.
Help them embrace
Your abundance, peace, and self-worth.
May they know their Truth and live it.
Indeed. And so it is.

My psychometric storyteller conveyed an inspiring message. The communication is loud and clear – no more unverified, third-world purchases, and no more unlaundered garments! I never thought such potent energy could transfer so casually. I'm still learning.

For my hardworking friends halfway around the globe, I'm sorry for your suffering. May failed research blossom into an opportunity, a connection through the ethers that uplifts and blesses. As my prayer permeates the astral plane – an urging for truth, recognition of value, and a call for self-care – may it reach you, my kindred spirits, and enrich your lives, if only just a little.

❖

Reflections

❖ *Has psychic energy ever told you a story? How has it impacted your life?*

❖ *What objects in your home have interesting information for you to explore?*

❖ *Have you ever received any impressions from them?*

❖ *Do you pray for others or send them positive and uplifting thoughts and energy? Can you recognize the love this offers to others?*

Tiny Toes

I can call spirits from the vasty deep.
~ William Shakespeare

Spirit, like God, denotes an object of psychic
experience which cannot be proved to exist in the
external world and cannot be understood rationally.
~Jung

I'm an animal lover and have been ever since childhood. Many furry, four-footed siblings who graced our home – Ace, Alfie, Samantha, Nikki, Kit, Simon, J.R., Arantxa, Kitty Girl – now occupy the spirit realm, all beloved friends and companions.

When I transitioned into a new life as a single mom, the adventure continued...

❖

It's spring 2008. The boys and I really want a dog, but the cost and time investment feel a bit daunting. Then again, knowing how important animals were to me as a child, how could I say no?

Enter Ash, a Lhasa Apso puppy, named by two Pokémon fans (aka our two boys Kaleb and Finn) after Ash Ketchum, the aspiring Pokémon trainer from the famous card game. Ash is the cutest fluffernutter ever. So much so that people can't help but stop to pet him. At five months he could be mistaken for a mop who lost its handle or a giant dandelion puffball. Basically, he's big eyes surrounded by wild fur that grows to the ground in long wavy-white weeds.

Traveling nearly everywhere with us, Ash is a great companion. He joins me at work, the store, on walks, and in the park. But when I leave him at home by himself, he seems lonely. Not for long.

Enter Zannah, named by Kaleb and Finn after a Sith Lord who turned from the dark side to the light.[36] Ash is none too impressed. He even tried to eat her on the way home from the breeder, but she's too tough and wiggly for consumption. Zannah continually pays him back for his transgression with her razor-sharp barking, the kind that splits ears and fractures glass. Ash may possess size and brute force, but Zannah's feminine stealth and powerful voice win every time.

---

[36] Darth Zannah was first identified by name in the magazine *Star Wars Helmet Collection 2.*

❖

The pups find their own way of teaching – two peeing-pooping-eating machines that bark, lick, and wag their way into our hearts. They demonstrate the power of unconditional love, help us grow patience, and encourage play. The boys are even learning about the birds and bees, as I don't have the heart to spay Zannah. (It seems much more painful and invasive than neutering, and perhaps, being a female, I feel for her in this.) As a result, every six months or so we encounter a lovely cycle of heat when Zannah makes Ash...well...her sex slave. (He's actually more willing than not.)

Embarrassing the boys many times in their two-week escapade, the furballs hump for hours until the sexually subordinate Ash, completely exhausted, threatens to eat her once again. (Not in a loving way, mind you.) Zannah, however, cannot be deterred. She bows to the goddess of creation with internal surges beyond her control, demanding service for days on end until the finale of her cycle. Then the dominatrix and her slave – deficient in necessary bodily fluids and absent adequate opposable thumbs to apply lube – get...well...stuck. Like a proverbial screwdriver in an electric socket, this embarrassing problem of immovable parts requires a power-down mode. In other words, said screwdriver must become less conductive through reabsorption of blood, if you catch my drift.

❖

Oh Lord, they're out in the yard again, advertising fun events at Casa D'Nicastro! Two dogs, precariously one, look like a freakishly-odd lawn ornament. Even the smarmiest of characters might blush. And while strangely entertaining, when a plumber scheduled to fix our broken toilet threatens to arrive during the Zannah-Ash-double-headed sex-monster – I panic.

Rushing to the freezer, I nervously drag ice compresses out and help the culprits cool down. *Oh, the miraculous shrinking effects of little frozen cubes!*

Luckily, Ash and Zannah quickly regain their standard two-dog status! *Praise Jesus!*

Crazy, awkward, and weirdly humorous, these events beautifully educate two young boys on the topic (and perhaps, even buy me stock in future birth control). Thank you, live nature channel!

Not long after Zannah arrives, Finn, our youngest, wants a cat. Both boys do, but I hear it most from Finn.

Ask, and the Universe delivers.

It's the fall of 2010. A Siamese kitten in the local shelter needs a loving home, so enter number one kitty.

Bu, short for Buddha, is the sweetest, most mellow kitty around. His casual transition from crate to home, facing two barking dogs, earns him the name. From a small gray transport into the midst of canine mayhem, his well-centered saunter went something like this:

Ash growls, "What the heck is that?"

"I don't know, but it's funny looking," barks Zannah.

Ash dances forward and backward, trying to poke it with his nose, the kind of jig meant for poisonous snakes and porcupines.

Zannah whines, "Oh my God, it might stay here!" realizing that this creature is, indeed, a new addition to the family.

"Over my dead body!" A serious stare from Ash attempts to threaten one tiny tan-and-black furball, too sweet to notice all the fuss.

Bu purrs – a feline Om that loves away all the fear.

Zen restored.

Bu is as cool as they come, a cool cat. Detached, unflappable, and always loving, he sits on Finn's shoulder to tour the house, takes "helicopter rides" in his baseball hat, and poses for the pussy paparazzi. (Yes, over and over, again.) Jackson loves to let him sleep in his bed, reassuring company to ward off monsters and scary things.

It's only two weeks since Bu joined the family, but he doesn't look well. A visit to the vet uncovers an infection, but the doctor suspects something graver is lurking.

We love this kitty that found his way here so quickly, so easily. Now, I begin to worry.

Another week has passed. Bu is even sicker, infected with what the doctor believes to be feline leukemia. We watch him eat, but no weight sticks, his feeble body shrinking in front of our eyes. He's losing his balance and has occasional accidents; so unusual for a cat, especially one so young.

There's nothing we can do, and I feel torn about putting him to sleep. Conflicted thoughts run through my brain, the alternate cycling of responsibility and the spiritual "rightness" of euthanizing.

It can't be long now.

The boys and I take turns. We hold him in a small basket, making him as comfortable as possible. We say prayers, urging him to leave this place and fly with the angels.

Tonight, Bu's breathing is short and raspy. His ravaged form lies weak and lifeless. Together, in my treatment room's calm and nurturing energy, the boys and I stand around him, weeping, knowing that death lurks in the corner. Calculated waiting.

As his frail body takes a final breath, I feel a bit relieved; he's escaped this heavy world. Kaleb swears he saw Bu's spirit leave as a tiny diamond light that lifted out of his body just as he stopped breathing. I believe him. There's much that Kaleb can "see."

This isn't the boys' first brush with physical death, having had many fish since they were toddlers. But Bu's passing feels different, something closer and even more personal, a fuzzy animal that wormed his way deep into our hearts.

We hold a homegrown funeral for our beloved fur baby. The boys carefully construct a little coffin for him from a shoebox, decorating the plain brown exterior with stickers and markers. Collecting gifts to help him make his journey to the other side, the boys find ways to honor their friend and heal their own hearts.

Gently placing Bu's fragile body on a tiny pillow, we close the box and take him outside, planting him among the flowers in a lovely bed of beautiful, pale pink peonies. The neighbors curiously look on as the three of us dig and cry, cry and dig.

He'll like it here, we say.

Finn and Kaleb have a deep bond with Bu; we all do. (I say have/do, present tense because this bond will never leave us, even though Bu has dumped that battered body.) And while Finn at times played with him a bit more, Kaleb takes his death in with such force that it seems to tear him apart.

Don't get me wrong; we all cry for Bu, but Kaleb weeps in long sobbing stretches. We sit in the kitchen, the living room, wherever he needs to be held while the pain passes through him. And in that space of loss and grief, by God's Grace, Bu gave Kaleb an unexpected blessing – the chance to process something profound and unfinished. It is a sacred offering, sent from one furry friend to his soul-brother – divinely planned, perfectly timed, and heart-healing.

We all miss Bu – his tiny little toes, soft round face, gentle eyes, and sweet demeanor. He undoubtedly misses us, too, because when the night's stillness blankets our bedrooms, he makes visits. Little cat toes gingerly walk up my leg, matching the pressure and sensation of Bu but missing the physical cat. Other times, the feeling of tender steps on my pillow around my ear alerts me to his presence.

With each visit Bu reminds us that he never ventured far, that he's just a thought, a memory, a heartbeat away. Most importantly, though, he taught us, again, the power of love. Some may say that he broke our hearts, but I say, "Not heartbroken, but a heart broken wide open." Bu came as a blessing, an incredible gift. There was not, nor ever has been, a cat more loved in such a short time.

We love you, Bu!

Reflections

- *What pets are/have been special to you? Why?*

- *What experiences with your pets offered you lessons? Gifts? Pride? Embarrassment?*

- *Has a pet's death come as a blessing, even with the challenges and pain of loss?*

- *Have any pets visited you after they passed over? How do you feel about their non-physical presence?*

Making Lemonade

It's not what happens to you, but how you handle it.
If Life gives you lemons, make lemonade.
If the lemons are rotten, take out the seeds
and plant them in order to grow new lemons.

— Louise Hay

One lesson we learn quickly on the spiritual path is this: traveling the mystical trail reveals many karmic events that call for resolution. Frequently, however, karma remains hidden from our conscious awareness and manifests mysteriously, coded within mind-boggling happenings, uncurable diseases, perplexing physical ailments, and tumultuous relationships that baffle us. All these signal that karma is afoot.

As you may already know, karma belongs to the Law of Cause and Effect.

Karma, a Sanskrit term, is the playing out of spiritual law — the lower energetic aspect of the Law of Cause and Effect. Remember, this Law holds that what we sow, we reap; whatever we put into the world comes back to us bigger and more potently than what we sent out in tandem with the Law of Attraction. Simply said, we are as responsible for our unloving thoughts, feelings, and actions as we are for the beauty that blooms from our grace-filled energy. The difference is merely a choice — a choice that only we can make.[37]

Because the nature of life is based on what-goes-around-comes-around energy, we draw to us loving gestures from our own compassionate deeds and goodwill, and create punitive karma from wrong-doing. In other words, we generate karma when we:

1) Believe that others have mistreated us and hold blame toward them;
2) Engage in abusive, disrespectful, and neglectful inter-actions, whether we feel guilty or not; and,
3) Believe we've wronged others through our words, thoughts, feelings, or deeds and stay anchored in blame, guilt, or anger with ourselves.

Unlike what you may think, the scope of "others" is quite broad, here. That means, looking beyond our day-to-day human interactions, unloving energy directed toward plant life, animals, and Mother Earth, is also a misuse of our power – the personal, energetic aspect of Intelligent Force in us – and one that holds a karmic price tag, too.

(Note: Animals do not have the same free will that we do. That is, their behavior falls in alignment with their nature. For example, there is no karma in the animal world for a lion eating a gazelle – a mutual survival-driven agree-

---

[37] Adriene Nicastro, *The Soul-Discovery Journalbook: An Intimate Journey into Self, Volume III.* (Bellefonte, PA: Pathways to Freedom Press, 2021), pp. 319-320.

ment between predator and prey. There is karma, how-ever, for humans shooting a lion in sport because it demonstrates a total disrespect for God's creatures, a need to control and possess; but a person who hunts deer with reverence, care, and gratitude for the animal to feed their family in need does not breed karma.)

As we expand karma's scope of influence once more, we can witness its effects on a larger scale. That is: because we are all connected through Sacred Unity, what we do to one is done to all. Like a pebble dropped in a pond, the ripples reach out in ever-increasing circles.

> Our lives are not our own. We are bound to others, past and present, and by each crime and every kind-ness, we birth our future.[38]

Thankfully, staying on the karmic cycle is a choice of our own making. In other words, we can choose to let go of blame and thus, transform the karma we created by recognizing it during our incarnation now, after passing, or a thousand lifetimes from now. Again, our choice.

So, how do we release karma? We can dissolve it by "paying back" to balance the scales or through forgive-ness. (We can also allow others to take on our karma for us or help us release it, but that's a whole other lesson.) When we open the door to peace and compassion – not necessarily approving or liking a negative act, but understanding it – that helps dispels our toxic emotions, allowing love to enter and permeate the situation. So, whether we feel owed, believe we owe another, or blame

---

[38] David Mitchell, *Cloud Atlas*.

ourselves, forgiveness breaks the karmic circle – forgive-ness extended to others and ultimately ourselves.[39]

I've dealt with my share of karma. Thankfully, I found the guidance to work with it, releasing myself and others from its toxic chains that bound me. And while I could share many a story, the following one rests quite potently in my mind…

It's October 2016, a tumultuous time. Custody changes top the list, but that's not the only challenge in my life. I've been creating a new workshop called *Colors of the Soul: Energetic and Spirit Connections for Healing.*

This workshop is one of many coming-out-of-the-healing-closet moments, teaching opportunities married with inspirational flashes of learning. I know that might sound wonderful, even growth-producing. Yet, the harbinger of what seems so promising is crushing fear.

Fear can sneak in, at first, with muddy footprints, sending clues of an intruder in my psyche. Dirty clues. At other times, dread (fear's big brother) sucker punches me in the solar plexus like a bully, leaving me bent-over, gasping for air.

What if I can't do this?

What if I shouldn't do this?

What if something awful happens because I'm doing this?

---

[39] For more on karma, see: Adriene Nicastro, *The Soul-Discovery Journal-book: An Intimate Journey into Self, Volume III.* (Bellefonte, PA: Pathways to Freedom Press, 2021), pp. 319-327.

These are the fretful questions that press on my mind – the remaining nervous threads of persecution as a Druid, a witch, a healer from other lifetimes; one part of me always sets off alarms to being known as a psychic or a healer. It rises when history threatens to repeat itself, looming thoughts about execution – another violent end to another journey in the flesh.

Putting materials together for my new workshop, a lovely addition to old fear shows its face. As I begin the practical steps of preparation, writing the slides to aid our discussion, my fervent focus is joined by a severe stabbing pain in my left glute – yes, one proverbial pain in the ass. As I stand from hours of computer time, a burning fuse of nerve bundles alights deep within the muscle. My butt is on fire...and not in a good way.

The discomfort continues to grow in intensity throughout the days of preparation for my teaching event, trying to eclipse the opening act of my stepping out. An awareness that this physical pain points to something more profound yet hidden doesn't elude me. Still, the stubborn teenager of my evolving psyche pushes onward, refusing to stop; long stretches of focused writing and planning dominate my time.

Decorating the extended periods of work are sporadic and unfruitful attempts to wipe out my discomfort. But it's as if all routes to healing the pain remain blocked. In other words, exploring its symbolism, ignoring it, stretching it, and chiropractic manipulation offer no relief. It won't submit; instead, the stabbing-knife sensation continues to grow and, alongside it, persistent fear and disquieting feelings, a shadow calling for stronger light.

Today is the workshop. This morning, flashes of past-life traumas fill the spaces between the Void and mental summersaults. Mere ideas about speaking up and being a healer conjure snippets from the depths of soul memory, filling my third eye with visions of physical death, punishment, execution. Violent treatment for a life well-intended. All of this threatens to invade the day, to stop me from teaching.

I need to teach. Time's up! Thoughts push and pull along with intense discomfort. The workshop starts in a few short minutes, yet pain grips my left side, trailing down my entire leg.

Plowing through discomfort – stand up, sit down, stand again – I bypass the yield signs with pigheaded determination, rejecting pain's dictates to rest and face this mysterious suffering with all that hides behind it.

The good news: I navigate the workshop without a hitch on the teaching side.

It's January, and the new year brings no relief. It's the mornings I now dread, anticipating the scalding wash of nerves on fire. They weep in silent screams while tiny cells of thigh, glutes, calf, and foot tear into invisible shreds.

At times all I can do is stand against a wall, breathing in short gasping gulps, hyperventilating until I feel high. Nothing works. I know the metaphysical whispers of something larger mumbles in the corners of my consciousness, but I can't make out the words.

One day seems to blend into the next as searing pain explodes from my sciatic nerve, radiating across my left cheek, around hip and thigh, all the way into the tip of my big toe. There's no more flesh to consume; it's burned clean by searing heat.

At least a name exists, an identity for the unidentifiable: a virus in the nerve. The only hurt to rival this agonizing ache – childbirth. But that ended after a mere twelve hours and blessed me with miraculous gifts. This lingers forever and produces nothing but pain.

I can't remember the last time I didn't hyperventilate through tasks, feeling like a burden to my husband as house duties and chores stack. Attempts to help myself result in nothing but self-harm, willful striving that increases my suffering. Mobility, ability, and simple self-care are impossible, and I must force myself to ask for help as toxic independence meets with pure necessity.

Suffice it to say, nothing else feels this humiliating. Nothing ever has. As I ask my husband to dress me, the agony of powerlessness hurts my heart and my silly pride.

I could hang around naked all day, but it's cold.

The weeks drag on. All activities, the ones where I feel more human, neatly fit into three upright actions –

showering, standing for ten-minute blocks, and walking down the hall or up the steps. Everything, and I mean *everything else*, I do on my back, including eating, reading, watching movies, meditating, seeing clients, and running groups. I still require assistance for many daily acts of living like dressing, meal prep, washing clothes, climbing into bed, etc. Driving the car, walking around the grocery store, taking out the dogs are out of the question.

Counterbalancing this minimal activity, waves of pain and discomfort match the swells of anxiety about the unmentionable; like a beach that waits for a tsunami, I, too, wait for my bladder or intestines to rise up and drown me in agony. I know it's a natural rhythm, one that's unavoidable. Still, I dread the surges of searing hurt, along with the bathroom itself. Most of all, it's a tie between the irritation of having to "go" (the exercise of getting there, sitting down, and staying as short as possible) *and* that bastard toilet. The hard seat scorches my skin, threatening to burn away layers of flesh to the bone.

Day after day, I pray, meditate, read, and reflect, searching for an answer. Resolution, however, feels non-existent or lost with the planes decorating the Bermuda Triangle's sandy bottom.

Maybe I'm not praying enough? Not reflecting enough?

The maybes continue to fill my thoughts.

Maybe I've done something so unforgivable...

As my attention draws to a single point, lessons begin to come into focus. Signposts label the belief in powerlessness, burdens, and loss, but the vaporous wisps lack detail; so I reach out with hope for help of another kind, to important teachers and healers.

One reading...

"This difficulty comes from a past life in which Dimitri was a king. [*Eye roll* – mine, of course.] In that lifetime, he was romantically interested in you, but another woman, your rival then and mother in this lifetime, wanted to be queen. Instead, Dimitri picked you, and the woman became so angry that she cursed you to '*never again sit in pleasure or power.*' You took in the curse as true, and this is why it's playing out."

In another past-life reading...

"You've had so many lifetimes of standing in your power and being punished for it, typically by death. But in at least one lifetime, Egyptian, you misused your power, which has excavated a fear."

Clarity is a powerful force. I rest moment by moment in a crystal-clear pool. It surges through me in uplifting waves, sacred healing energy that carries me inward and upward, a very slow but steady shift from the previous weeks.

Spiritual literature, journaling, meditation, prayer – this is my job, my only job now. This and rest, a challenging task for me.

Dimitri is terrified that I've ruptured a disc or worse. To ease his fear, I schedule a trip to an orthopedic doctor. But even the physician had no diagnosis to offer. Nothing gained.

All attempts, in fact, to find medical answers have run head-on into brick walls, a sure sign of karma afoot. Alternative options like acupuncture only aggravate my condition. And another stab at mainstream intervention, through my primary care physician, results in the same. No insight. His solution – a prescription for muscle relaxants. Nothing is less appealing than the idea of being a painfilled, immobilized drooling blob.

Instead, I turn to the Ultimate Doctor.

I'm on an upward swing, able to walk around the house for longer periods. This is heaven compared to the past weeks, and I feel less confined. Less powerless. Sitting is still problematic for extended periods, but in the short run, possible for small chunks of time.

I make my way into the kitchen for a snack, stopping at the center barnwood island; it provides a welcome station, a place to pause as I stand mindfully and step away from work. The searing sciatic shocks, lower in intensity, feel like a break, too. The marathon breathes.

As I pause, something altogether different comes to my attention – intense groin pain, piercing muscles in an utterly distinctive way. Immediately, reminders of both pregnancies surface, the times when pelvic ligaments stretch and ache under the strain of baby feet pushing uterine walls, jumping on my pelvic floor like a trampoline.

Curiously, this aching has company – bubbles of unconscious awareness rising to the surface, threatening to break my momentary peace. The fragile iridescent spheres house powerful energy, a cutting fusion of emotion and sensation tagged as unfinished parenthood. They float into my mind, bursting on gray matter while alerting my solar plexus to crushing loss – pain, pregnancy, birthing, death, and a sense of failure. Like a piece of broken glass too fragmented to fix, the unseen brings past to present in one devastating blow.

I must have been abandoned in another lifetime when I was pregnant. This thought is so potent it strips away my breath, a sudden gasp to collapse lungs. With it a portal opens and through the doorway, visions from a life long ago, a soul memory, rush into the space...

I am walking through the woods, walking with purpose, as fast as I can. The autumn leaves litter the forest floor in a blanket of dry brown parchment that crunches in protest under my feet. To the left, a stream, lined with smooth burnt umber pebbles, opposes a thick forest to the right. Shadows of dense underbrush make the landscape seem unwelcoming. Many trees already stand bare, stark taupe arms reaching into a cloudy, gray sky. Calling. Searching. They point to something greater, yet I feel alone.

Looking down, I follow the lines of my body. A short gray cloak keeps in the heat, a welcome buffer from the cool fall air. A rounding at my abdomen threatens to expose what I keep hidden, a weight sitting deep within my center.

I am pregnant...pregnant and alone in the woods.

The baby will be born here, safe from judging eyes.

I seek the shelter of trees. A sacred circle of evergreens nestled in the wild protect me and this unborn child.

I squat. *The baby's coming.*

Young, very young, a Puritan teen lost to myself and my community, I trust no one. Fear and suspicion dominate my life.

They'll stone me.

And the baby? Probably an offering to the river.

Instead, I rest here in the arms of our beloved Mother. She holds me now in leaves and moss and earth.

The babe is borne.

Suddenly, my focus shifts. I cut with stone, then teeth, and stone again. The lifeline that connected us remains, just not in the flesh. He is silent in my task. Blue and cold. Only stillness, not of peace, survives; it's stagnant and hollow. My heart, heavy.

I dig. The ground is chilly, and the air tastes like decaying leaves. Hands expose pungent soil, rich and fertile.

A shallow grave is all that I can offer...all I can provide this child, a child who won't be held, who won't nuzzle or feed at my breast, or play. I'll not watch him seek a mate or meet his own children.

I weep.

At least he's safe and warm, clothed in blankets of velvety green and rich brown. Held by Her just like She holds me.

Searching for a rock large enough to end our silent ceremony, I find a moss-covered gray one. *This will have to do.* My hand lingers as I mark his place – a nest for his tiny body while his spirit soars.

Rest in peace, my sweet angel.

As the vision stops, grief takes its place, a tidal wave that threatens to drown me where I stand. While I struggle to move out of its path, my feet remain frozen to the cold tile floor.

Heart-wrenching cries escape my throat as the feeling of the unfinished parenthood claws its way to the surface, tearing through my insides with such force I bend to its will. Like a half-sculpted masterpiece, barren mother-arms grasp at air; what was once filled with life, is replaced by aching emptiness.

A breathless thought breaks the vortex that makes our kitchen spin. *This groin pain at least has a source, a mystery solved.* I know without question that it harkens to pregnancy, a full womb, ligaments stretched and aching – a reminder of being a vessel for life and all that comes with that beautiful package, even the heartache.

Still, clarity never felt so hollow. Instead, remnants of sadness rest in this void and threaten to swallow me whole – divorce, custody changes, loss, and regret – lingering in the vision's wake.

I breathe. That's enough for now.

❖

The intensely uniting nature of mother and child moves well past time and space. It manifests beyond the temporal and into the unseen, in this way. First, on a physical level connected by flesh, the bearer of life sustains through the umbilical cord's nurturing structure, the lifeblood of mother to child. At birth we sever this cord so our offspring can live as a "separate" human being. However, all things physical possess etheric, mental, emotional, and spiritual counterparts. So, even though we cut the physical cord, an etheric one – a copy of the corporal and bridge to our higher bodies – remains fully intact and visible with psychic eyes. Mentally and emotionally, it signifies a bond in thoughts and feelings – the desire to nurture, care for, support, and love, *and* the child's love for the parent regardless of circumstances. Spiritually, it symbolizes our connectedness and everlasting lifeline with Source, absent only in our awareness.

I know the echoes of that long-ago motherhood, of that lost child. He lingers in my soul calling to be heard and remembered, one shadow to my current struggles, a harbinger of regret and grief.

Tangled timelines present priceless gifts.

What gift could come from such pain? Forgiveness. And the gift of eternal memory, for as many times as I need to hear it...

Love is never, ever lost.

When life hands us lemons, we have a choice: to make lemonade and relish the beauty of our lessons, or to repeat and suffer.

I make lemonade whenever my being calls for it. There's nothing so sweet as the release of hurt into nothingness and taking in the love that remains.

And so, dear reader, I offer you a grace-filled and healing blessing in honor of this chapter, an ancient Uto-Aztecan prayer for forgiveness, affection, detachment, and liberation:

Ancient Nahuatl Blessing

I release my parents from the feeling
that they have already failed me.

I release my children from the
need to bring pride to me; that they may
write their own ways according to their hearts, that
whispers all the time in their ears.

I release my partner from the obligation
to complete me. I do not lack anything;
I learn with all beings all the time.

I thank my grandparents and forefathers who have
gathered so that I can breathe life today. I release them
from past failures and unfulfilled desires, aware that
they have done their best to resolve their situations
within the consciousness they had at that moment. I
honor you; I love you, and I recognize you as innocent.

I am transparent before your eyes, so they know that I do
not hide or owe anything other than being true to myself
and to my very existence, that walking with the wisdom
of the heart, I am aware that I fulfill my life project,
free from invisible and visible family loyalties that
might disturb my Peace and Happiness,
which are my only responsibilities.

I renounce the role of savior, of being one
who unites or fulfills the expectations of others.
learning through, and only through, LOVE,

I bless my essence, my way of expressing,
even though somebody may not understand me.
I understand myself, because I alone
have lived and experienced my history;
because I know myself, I know who I am,
what I feel, what I do and why I do it.
I respect and approve myself.

I honor the Divinity in me and in you.

We are free.

A side note: At the start of autumn, when leaves littered
the ground and the air turned cold, sudden histamine
overload would manifest into intense asthma. Metaphysically, asthma and breathing issues represent feeling
unworthy of taking in the Breath of Life or Divine Breath.
In the autumn following this chapter's past-life healing,

the fall asthma, which plagued me every year for as long as I can remember, never surfaced. The seasonal trauma – erased from soul memory through forgiveness, dissolving my karma – was transformed.

❖

Reflections

❖ *Have you ever experienced a feeling so strongly about something, a harkening to a time and place disconnected from now? Might something in this story help explain your experience?*

❖ *If you've been aware of past-life resonance, what has it come to offer? To teach? What gift has it given you?*

❖ *Is it possible to consider that any of your discomfort, symptoms, or disease states have roots in something beyond your current awareness?*

❖ *What beliefs, thoughts, or emotions might your current symptoms/health issues be pointing to?*

❖ *What karma might still exist in your life? What guilt, blame, or resentment could point to it?*

Cord Surgery

Life is everything. Life is God.
Everything shifts and moves,
and this movement is God.
And while there is life, there is delight
in the self-awareness of the divinity.
- Leo Tolstoy

After many years of study, I've come to see Source – God, Great Spirit, Allah, or whatever you want to call the Divine – in everything and everyone. Some days I feel wholly centered in this vision, knowing and feeling that Cosmic Presence infuses my world. But other days, it's more challenging.

Leaping off my good days, I understand that all things work beautifully, a reflection and emanation of Divine energy. That is to say, this world (macro and micro) is a masterpiece meant to operate in perfect order - our bodies, nature, and even our creations. Nothing is exempt.

Healing, then, is the recognition of our Divine center radiating through us. This happens as we rest in intimate union with Source through the vibration of Love.

Love, unconditional and pure Love, dissolves the blockages that keep anything or anyone from existing in wholeness. For this we must look beyond the earthly vision of personality and state of perceived separation held by our ego-mind to the image that Source has of us – always perfect, always precious, always whole.

Healing can take many forms; however, the broadest and most far-reaching includes prayer and spiritual energy healing. That may surprise many readers because physical interventions like medicine or mental and emotional treatment like psychotherapy are the norm where restorative practices are concerned. It goes without saying that a broken arm may still need a cast and that the psychologically distraught may benefit from counseling; yet, I never discount the value and transformative power of the spiritual and esoteric to promote health and return us to wellness.

While spiritual healing and prayer may seem easier to consider for humans, animals, and even plants, applying these practices to man-made inventions could raise a serious eyebrow for many.

That said, I'll take the risk anyway, walking out on a tenuous limb. Here goes...

Everything benefits from prayer and spiritual energy healing. Everything. This includes plants, birds, bugs, fish, and Mother Earth. We can also invite the non-fleshy, breathless occupants of our world – automobiles, computers, and other machines – to operate in the perfection with which they were created, calling forth the God-energy in them to align in perfect working order.

I can almost hear your thoughts, an understandable mixture of some doubt and bits of confusion. God in a car? Source in a computer? Healing our contraptions with anything but screwdrivers or pliers? Utterly crazy!

Please just put your questioning brain on pause for a moment and consider this: Where can you keep out the Cosmic Energy of Source? Where do you think God is absent?

The answer is NOWHERE. God is an ever-present force that infuses everything, and here is how:

Love is the source of all creation. It is the very hub upon which existence in form takes place. Love is the cohesive Power of the Universe and without Love, a Universe could not be. Love is that powerful!

In the science world love expresses itself as the attractive forces between electrons. ...The electron is pure Light or Spirit of God, the Creator. It remains forever uncontaminated, self-contained, and indestructible. If it wasn't so it could not obey and fulfill the Law (The Great Cosmic Law of Life). The Law is the directing activity of Love. The only True substance, out of which all things are made, the Perfect Life Essence of God.[40]

---

[40] Rev. Penny Donovan, *Moonlight Wisdom: Night Lessons from My Teachers.* (Albany, NY: Sacred Garden Fellowship, 2018), pp. 11-12.

So, despite what you may believe, machines hold creative energy, too. And the same Creative Force that ignites us infuses anything we make – a combination of sacred energy from the person who created it and God-energy held in the natural materials used for its construction.

I understand your hesitation, your questioning. I'd be a doubting Thomas, too, without the spiritual teachings from Sacred Garden Fellowship and real-life examples from my beloved teacher Rev. Penny. You see, Penny re-started her car after the battery "died" in the middle of a big snowstorm. I'm not talking about screwdrivers and jumper cables here, though using tools would be a form of healing, too. She had no time to wait for mechanical assistance with dangerously plummeting temperatures and the deepening night. Instead, she used spiritual energy healing and prayer, calling on the Cosmic Force to reanimate and repair.

Sounds crazy? Crazy like a fox, maybe.

I guess you'll just have to make up your own mind on this one...

I'm on my way out the door to meet a day filled with errands. In the next hour, I planned a telephone meeting en route, multitasking as usual. For this, a well-charged cell phone will do the job, but I know said phone is low in power. So, I grab a charging cord and its accompanying portable battery, which sit unassumingly in an antique wooden cheese box near the garage.

Hopefully, the tiny black portable charging block will save me – a guarantee of power – if the car's phone adaptor is missing in action. Still, I know this very charging cord can be a bit unpredictable. It is, however, my only option.

In a hurry with tasks and calls on my mind, I climb into my car with phone, cord, and portable cube in hand. Preparing, I plug the phone into the charging block. All settled. Satisfied, I back out the driveway and turn toward downtown.

With my phone neatly juicing as a small passenger next to me, I feel ready for the day, but a niggling thought presses, *Why deplete the battery?* So, I scrounge through the car's nooks and crannies, thankfully discovering the phone adaptor that's carefully tucked in the center console. Pulling the plug on the existing charging block to connect the USB into its new power source, my preparation for this afternoon's meeting feels complete.

As the cord clicks into the phone's port, I patiently wait for the tiny lightning bolt, the one that will announce with a quiet ding, *Phone charging!* But nothing. Plug again. Nothing. Okay, plug again. Ten times I plug in the bloody cord – the same fashion when it peacefully charged in the portable battery on my car seat – but not a single electron must be reaching its destination.

Fine. I'll plug it back in the portable battery, an agitated attempt to solve the problem.

So I place the flat USB head into the charging block, again, hoping. But nothing. And again. Nothing. Now I risk having no battery just before my important phone call. *Ugh!*

Suddenly a lightbulb explodes in my head! *Why...not... heal it? If Penny can energetically heal her car battery, I can heal this ornery cord!*

Parking the car to prevent any further catastrophes, (You didn't think I was really going to do this driving, did you?) I begin, as I always do – with a prayer and setting of intent, knowing that Divine energy is ever-present and available for service.

Dear Mother-Father God,
Thank you for this opportunity
to call forth Your Sacred Flow
and transform this cord on all levels.
I envision it working in perfect order,
as it was created.
I know You hear me as You always do.
Indeed. And So, It Is.

Open to the movement of energy, I sit in stillness as a rush of power travels through my core like a warm, electric waterfall – the small stream matched in strength to the task at hand.

Now for the test. I plug the phone in and...Nothing. No lightning bolt. No ding.

Okay, let me pause here for a moment to ask. Are you disappointed? Or are you thinking, of course, silly, you can't do that?

Well, the story doesn't end there. I refuse to allow my ego a victory. Here we go, again.

I stand strong, centered in my intent and open to the energy, as a recognition of power in my Self surfaces. A familiar feeling flushes quickly through my core, a charged rush deep within. Now, for the moment of truth.

With the charger in hand, I plug the small black Micro-USB connector into the phone. "Ding!" A truly happy sound as the lightning bolt appears on the screen to announce, "I'm charging!"

"It worked!" I squeal just loud enough to be embarrassing. The sing-song voice of my four-year-old self chimes, "I healed the cord! I healed the cord!" *Yep, but don't let ego sneak in there with arrogance.*

"Thank you, God," I offer out loud as a smile washes over my face.

Of course, it worked! The second time, that is. Did you doubt that it would? If you did, that's okay. Clearly, I wondered a bit myself. This experience, though, helped me move one step closer to total trust.

Remember, everything is made of Divine energy. Everything. Each molecule in our world vibrates with the same power that creates oceans, plants, and people. It can be channeled through another, who uses the energy to produce machines, pencils, and books, or it can be offered as healing.

The Divine aspect of form expresses communion with our shared God-energy. Through faith, we all can claim our state of wholeness, even the little black charging cords of the world.

Reflections

❖ *Where do you "see" Source?*

❖ *Can you change your mind and heart to witness Source in everything? Why or why not?*

❖ *Could you imagine a change in your life if you began to see the world with Divine energy all around you, in you, in all things, even inanimate objects? How?*

❖ *How did this chapter influence your thinking about healing?*

❖ *What areas of your life would you like to change through healing?*

Heart Healing

*The wound is the place
where the Light enters you.*

~ Rumi

Within us lies a calling, innate to our Spirit and distinctively ours. Whether it's art, architecture, medicine, math, or other areas of study – the particular focus remains inconsequential, except for our growth and development. In other words, regardless of where we are drawn, we always land precisely where we need to be.

I must caution you, though. Let's not deceive ourselves, thinking that one calling is better than another. Everything we do, when we come from our Divine center, is a gift. So, whether you clean homes, treat clients, care for children, teach classes, or deliver mail, anything done with love and compassion – as a way of being your Self in the world – is a valuable and honorable offering to the Cosmic flow of life.

A passion, a hobby, a career, or service to the world... these are the ways Spirit draws us onward and upward, to express the pure love energy of Source from our Self through our self. The magnetic pull to a particular occupation, area of expression, or topic of intense study emerges from several lifetimes of practice as our calling infuses and informs our life purpose, echoing the cycles and patterns of this earth-plane journey. So, whatever you're doing now, however you feel drawn to it, repeats itself from previous incarnations into the now.

As the desire to fulfill our life plan brings any calling to fruition, we derive great benefit from the experience, and it is this: when we genuinely love what we're doing, it doesn't feel like work. Instead of being tiresome or monotonous, it feeds us on all levels, and in turn, we can give back naturally, effortlessly, and most importantly with love.

This is how I arrived in the healing arts, lured like a moth to the light. The path, however, has been a winding road filled with many lessons and experimentation along the way. Nonetheless, a spark became a flame, and with it a deep desire to understand, know, and help others heal themselves.

Through the years, I investigated many avenues of the healing arts – modern medicine, herbal remedies, nutrition, psychology, and spiritual healing – either by practice, study, or both, to land just where I was meant to be with each step of my journey. (We all arrive at the same place – where we were meant to land.)

With my studies, I became intimately schooled in wounding as well as healing. With each phase, my understanding grew – nutritionally, then psychologically, and finally spiritually.

At first, my focus centered on the physical level – alternative healing for disease states of humankind. Then I shifted toward injuries to the psyche: the pain behind challenging events, situations, and traumas, as well as the toxic emotions and unhealthy thoughts that can fracture minds or turn-tail and wreak havoc in the body. But as my learning shifted to the spiritual, previously held notions that we *generate* all injuries via our physical form changed monumentally. Why? Because metaphysics explained, with exacting detail, our belief systems in action and the reasons behind any physical issue.

What continues to amaze me is the spiritual map of our healing, particularly how all injury/disease appears quite different to the naked eye, altogether altered from its actual cause. How liberating to find that a slip of a knife, a car accident, the flu, or cancer (or any other "disease" or "dis-ease") must first exist in our mental body as a blockage to Truth, a limiting belief about ourselves or our world. This is a fundamental lesson in the realm of spiritual healing and certainly a way to extricate ourselves from the prison built by a god of fate or a hostile universe. (Freeing, but sometimes quite frustrating, knowing where my responsibility lies!)

I wholeheartedly love being a healer on all the levels in which I endeavor to work with clients. To be part of healing is a gift to the healee AND the healer – giving and receiving as one.[41] And even though I greatly desire to

---

[41] "...the completeness of giving and receiving only occurs as giving and receiving become one. As such, giver and receiver join perfectly like the pieces of a puzzle nesting in one another to create a whole. While we may witness this union in many ways, a common example can be experienced through the wholehearted exchange of a present – the giver lovingly gives while receiving the blessing of giving and feeling the receiver accept, and the receiver accepts and blesses the giver with love, giving in return through gratitude." *Adriene Nicastro, The Soul-Discovery*

describe the feelings of my experiences, no words will ever suffice, like communicating a profoundly personal love affair, tragedy, or mystical happening to another, precisely as we felt it. Even the most descriptive words lack the essence and energy to allow others to feel our feelings. What I can offer, though, is another story about healing, hopefully imparting the enriching, grace-filled, and loving nature of it, if only just a little.

As part of my ongoing healing practice and study, I hold sacred circles – a gathering of like-minded individuals who desire to call forth the wholeness in others and themselves through spiritual energy healing. For our group, this work happens with hands just above or lightly on the person's body (frequently behind the neck at the base of the skull) to transmit energy to the healee, who uses it (quite subconsciously) to clear blockages, release mental struggles, ease pain, and/or facilitate cellular regeneration.[42]

The group typically works with one another. Upon request, we host others who desire to heal, accommodating them either remotely or in person. The following is an account of one such circle in which we sent healing to one of our group members, an experience that touched each of us deeply.

---

[42]All healing occurs by accepting the Presence, the unconditional love of Source that clears away anything that doesn't serve us. This occurs organically as we surrender, open, and awaken to That which lies within us – God healing us by working through us.

It's spring 2018. Circle is tonight, but Felicia cannot attend. She struggles with significant back pain, the kind that has kept her supine in bed for days. Unable to drive, she intends to participate in remote healing by lying down in a quiet space at home. Simultaneously, another person physically present in the group will "sit in" for her – a conduit to transmit the energy, acting as Felicia. This brings Felicia present within the group beyond any perceived limits of time and space.

To facilitate this healing, we will join in a heartfelt connection, resting in union with Felicia. Envisioning her through "spiritual eyes" as whole and perfect, we will allow the fullness of spiritual healing energy to flow through each of us and into her for restoration.

You see, healing is not bound by time and space. It can go where we direct it, through our Divine connection, beyond geographic separation or the dictates of a clock. The group can send healing to anyone, living anywhere, at any time, just as we all intend with Felicia.

Opening the group in a typical fashion, I begin with a prayer – a heartfelt thanks to Spirit, angels, Master teachers, and Source for guidance, love, and support. We follow with a brief meditation to raise our consciousness in preparation for the work before us. Then with an intentional pause, an inner knowing informs us of how to lead the healing and determine who will sit in for Felicia.

The pull or inspiration anyone experiences to be a conduit for another is entirely personal. Additionally, Divine helpers coordinate a mutual healing experience for the person sitting-in and the healee, an opportunity for those being healed to take in understanding that the conduit (sit-in) already knows.

For me, receiving as a sit-in comes as an energetic tug in my heart. Today, I feel drawn to help Felicia in this way. For now, the reason remains unknown, but I am clear this is the task before me; so I trust that any reasons behind these Spirit urgings will become apparent soon.

Making contact via phone, Felicia tells us she is ready. She's resting in bed, a familiar place for her these past days.

I lay down on our healing table (a massage table in another life) and connect – heart to heart, soul to soul, and Spirit to Spirit. The group stands around me on all sides of the table. Through prayer and intent, we rest as one heart, one mind with Source, and envision Felicia as whole – embracing and accepting her natural state as a Divine Child.

Lying on the table connected with Felicia, I feel the energy rush through my whole body like cool water. It pulses with distinct potency. A heaviness in my chest, the weight of thick choking grief, not my own, begins to slowly dissolve in the rich, electric essence that cleanses and clears, gently soothing.

Filled with visions, colorful images play like movies projected from my third eye. I see Felicia kneeling at a grave, pounding the ground. Swearing. Yelling. Cursing at God. She pleads with a wave of fierce, grief-filled anger. A pained "why?" escapes from her tightened jaw, demanding answers from a god that feels deaf to her.

"Why did he need to pass?" This is the question that presses on her consciousness, fueling an epic meltdown.

The images change, and I lie in a death shroud – my body on a cold, stone slab covered with a thin white cloth. A little boy walks around me from the spirit world, pulling at the gossamer material that signifies (his mother Felicia's) metaphorical passing.

"Don't die. Please don't die, Mommy," cries the child, begging Felicia to not die to herself or others, consumed by grief.

This request is a calling from the spirit of her deceased child, a plea to let go of the pain and to not emotionally pass away with him. This visitor from beyond wants to let his mom know that she let a part of herself leave through his death, a part of her that she needs to heal in order to move on.

The vision changes, yet again – a flash of a woman rocking a baby. She sings *By Baby Bunting.* I hear the words from the song in my head...*Bye baby bunting, daddy's gone a-hunting, to by a little rabbit skin, to wrap the baby bunting in.*

The healing ends and with it, the heaviness in my chest and throat. The rest of my body vibrates, a buzzing that signals radiant power doing its work.

Our group calls Felicia via phone, offering impressions and messages from the healing, a typical closure to the process. This opportunity finalizes the healee's transformation through compassionate words and inspirational wisdom. I mindfully describe my experience as a sit-in, carefully recounting what I saw and felt – the anger, the grave, the death shroud, the grief, the loss of self, the baby being rocked. Felicia listens intently.

Verifying all that we share, she says, "Everything you described is exactly what happened! The problem started this week when my grandchild came down with the flu and launched me into intense worry. I found myself thinking about Samuel and feared I would lose my grandchild, too." (Felicia lost Samuel, who died as a small child.)

"I visited Samuel's grave, crying, yelling, and feeling very angry at God. I wanted to know why this happened! Afterward, I spent days in bed, filled with very intense fear. My low back hurt so badly that I couldn't move, and I did feel like part of me died."

The confirmation profoundly touched the group, a feeling difficult to explain. Yet, I am so very grateful for the experience and the opportunity to be a vessel for healing.

One unsolved piece remained – the song and woman rocking at the end of the healing. As my mind seeks answers, an intuitively-fueled sense slides in from the side. It is a thought, not my own, offered to close the loop.

"Felicia, did you have intense low back pain and sharp aching in your groin ligaments during your pregnancy with Samuel?"

"Hmmm...Yes. Yes, I did. Why?"

"Was it the same kind of pain you experienced this week?

"Come to think of it, yes!"

"Because the song didn't make sense until now. The mother rocking a child and singing a nursery rhyme informs the source of your back pain. I experienced the same while shedding the grief of custody changes – intense back and groin pain mimicking those during pregnancy – linked to my own feelings of lost motherhood. Your low back and groin pain was a reminder of your pregnancy and the loss associated with Samuel's death. It's what you've released in this healing along with your anger at God, the feeling of great grief, and fear that it could happen again, sparked by your grandson's flu."

"Remember Felicia, love is never lost."

Now I know why Spirit guided me to be a sit-in for Felicia. My intimate connection with similar lessons and related pain allowed the message to flow through me as a reminder. I know it well.

Thank you, Felicia. Thank you, boys. Thank you, Bringer of Light.

This is the power of healing. The energy, the prayer, the intention, and loving guidance from spirit and Spirit.[43] Giving and receiving unified, experienced, and expressed by all. My, how blessed we are!

---

[43] The distinction between lower case spirit versus upper case Spirit is meant to signify the energy of those who passed (spirit) as compared to the energy of Source (Spirit).

❖

Reflections

❖ *Have you experienced the healing power of prayer, spiritual energy healing, or spirit messages?*

❖ *Have you found healing by supporting and loving others through their challenges?*

❖ *What experiences of others helped you heal your own pain?*

❖ *Has the death of a loved one profoundly touched your life? How?*

Miracles in Weis

*This is my simple religion. There is no need for temples;
no need for complicated philosophy. Our own brain,
our own heart is our temple; the philosophy is kindness.*

~ Dalai Lama

Public outings provide many occasions to witness ourselves through others – allowing our human-ness, judgments, and helpful or not-so-helpful attitudes to play out. The reactions and interactions to/ with everyone can tell us much about ourselves and how we see the world. If used constructively, many growth opportunities surface, like all situations of living in relationship.

One of my favorite places for such learning happens in grocery stores. There we can watch fellow shoppers meander through boxes of cereal and pounds of vegetables, fight with their children, and nearly drown in the depths of decisions – the more obvious and pedes-trian supermarket events. However, hidden behind the curtain of our conscious awareness, this landscape holds an unseen cloud of energy. Swirling within any space, for that matter, is an invisible vibrational pool made from objects (living and non-living), people, and the relation-ships between and among everything and everyone. In other words, any store "climate"– formed from those working, those passing through as shoppers or suppliers, as well as the building, products, and produce, acted upon and interacted with – combines and compounds to become the site's amalgamated energy.

As an empath, teacher, and person doing spiritual work, opportunities within the marketplace lie in several areas. Perhaps most significant is the management and protec-tion of my energy, the desire to navigate shopping with-out being bombarded by mass consciousness or others' attitudes/energy. Why? Because the vibration of crowds and stores presses on me as a weight, mixing with emotions and thoughts hanging in the nearby ethers, a multi-sensory wonder (or a cloud of contamination, depending on how you want to see it). At other times, the energy of heavily populated places overwhelms me, and I'd rather hide. And sometimes, the earth-based "feed-your-body" tasks just seem too taxing. However, once I navigate any initial resistance, staying centered to avoid negative energy while reacting lovingly to what I see or witness becomes the overarching goal.

Bringing a loving consciousness into action takes focus and dedication, and provides fascinating day-to-day liv-ing. One such story says it best...

I find myself, once again, stocking up, a typical stop at Weis between work and the arrival of two starving boys. Scanning this local grocery hub, a day like any other, I walk among shelves packed with boxes, cans, packages, and bins of produce. I watch parents hurry cranky children through "crack-filled" checkout lines while elderly folks ration their weekly funds, carefully weighing options of necessary vs. unnecessary – a loaf of bread, one quart of milk, two apples, etc. Put the flavored iced tea back!

Finishing the last of my mad food dash, I approach a checkout line empty enough to make the wait brief. Standing near the magic black conveyer belt, my eyes scan a colorful magazine display that keeps me company with outlandish and humorous headlines, ones that make me shake my head.

Suddenly, inescapable noise breaks my state of peace and mild amusement with aura-cracking shrieks, sounds that pervade all my faculties. They ricochet off the scuffed linoleum floor like fractured glass shards threatening to puncture anything nearby. No one could miss the immense turmoil that rapidly fills this otherwise casually busy space.

Surveying the nearby checkout lines, my eyes and ears magnetically move to the source, raucous noise that continues to emanate from two figures sending shock waves into the ethers. Carefully observing, I can see them move through their checkout line and step into full view, three aisles away – first, the howling child, then the screaming parent in alternating outbursts that sometimes blend with competing discordant shrieking.

The sum total of my attention feels transfixed, hijacked by loud, gut-wrenching sobs from the young girl. The parent – a now thunderous, impatient mother – berates and criticizes so gruffly that only the completely deaf and blind might escape this painful scene.

Trying, as I might, to mind my business and stay center-ed – a highly empathic woman on a necessary mission – my heart can't help but instantly reach out to this grief-stricken little girl. Unlike a standard tantrum, her cries seem welded with heartbreak, an audible soul trauma impossible to ignore. As empathic resonance morphs us into energetic twins, her agony becomes mine: I hear my mother in her mother, me in her.

A growing angst, mixed with irritation, fills the space between us. *If this mother behaves like this in public, I fear even more for this child's psyche at home.*

Watch your thoughts, a mindful brainwave breaks through my overwhelmed state. Immediately, I know that my empathy risks contamination from judgment and contempt. A vital choice remains before me – use all my spiritual tools or continue to see a cruel mother hurting her child, a malicious parent and a victimized daughter.

In truth, I don't know what has happened or transpired prior to the event to cause such behavior in each of them. Stress, tiredness, irritability, a complicated history – their shared timeline is a mystery. What I do know is this: the interaction is toxic, but no clear public abuse is happen-ing to warrant intervention or for this to be my business. Still, my heart sits on mounting concern.

I must do something for them both and for myself, something to help soothe the situation.

This is, actually, a great opportunity – a chance to practice my spiritual tools – to avert criticism, judgments, and involvement that may potentially escalate the situation. So, a silent spiritual approach becomes my intent and the gentlest option.

Breathe and step out of the energy. Air, meant to calm, travels in through my nose, and I exhale with purpose.

Now for the shift: *How can I see this mother differently? Her daughter?*

As I approach the register, I continue to breathe mindfully, deeply, changing my thoughts as I watch the two. Mother still brashly yells while her daughter cries uncontrollably, en route to a bench at the end of their register.

Only an open heart can be helpful; so, all focus goes there, to my heart center, to heart-mind, cultivating a sense of peace and reaching into unconditional love. Different thoughts need to replace the old, not through linear, concrete figuring but with a higher awareness that knows truth. This mother suffers pain, a pain she passes onto her child, but that vision must be met with understanding, transformed by calling on the mother's kind-heartedness and love that rests deep within her.

Still watching from afar, I actively let go of my little self, the ways it wants to witness this mother as broken. Instead, I "see" her with compassion, recognizing her personality as a soul on a journey. Silently connecting heart-to-heart, I observe her as temporarily struggling, while the eternalness of her remains filled with the innate love of Spirit, an ever-present love that merely waits for expression.

Consciously feeling love for the mother from my Spirit, my Christ, the love that she cannot seem to express for herself or her daughter, I wrap her and her precious child in light.

With a sense of peace, joy, and unconditional Christ love, I pack the last bag in my cart.

The shift comes instantaneously, a very different sight apart from all that just transpired. It begins with a smile and a hug for her daughter, a sense of growing harmony between them and a calm silence in their demeanor, visible and palpable from aisles away.

Pushing my cart, I move toward the store exit. As I amble toward their bench, my eyes meet with the mother, and she catches my connection. I smile. She smiles back. Two souls, in time but out of time, share a moment beyond words. A beautiful and profound heartfelt recognition passes between us.

> I see you.
> I am here![44]

For the first time in my active memory, I consciously feel the eternal love within us, that *is* us – Christ love. Expressed as the Christ Consciousness, we see God in all. No judgment, no anger...only love.

Dare I say that I changed this situation? That what I did, shifted the energy? No, not my little personality self. The change came from the power of unconditional love.

This is the nature of love. Love has the power to dissolve anything negative, a light that shines away all darkness. A shift in mother, a shift in child, a shift in me is from love. Union opened the door to a miracle, a miracle in Weis.

How could a shift in me even make an impact? Is that arrogance, ignorance, self-importance? It could be com-

---

[44] This traditional Zulu greeting symbolizes mutual recognition of Divine Essence in humankind; as the greeted and greeter respond to one another, they "see" their authentic Selves.

ing from the little self, but this is not the source of which I speak. The movement, the change, comes from the love of God as the Christ, from the Self of us that extends authentic feeling, compassionate thoughts, healing words, or a warm embrace. And with our spiritual vision, the transformative action of Divine Love calls the same forth in another – vibrating twin violin strings playing the sacred music within us.

We are One, intimately and eternally connected, impacting each another in ever-increasing ripples.

Love moves mountains.

Reflections

❖ *Is there a time when you've felt love for another beyond the logic that calls for reprimand or punishment?*

❖ *Can you find opportunities to drop your judgments and instead choose love and compassion for others? For yourself?*

❖ *What must you let go of to live with and in unconditional love, peace, and joy?*

Dis Gon B'Gud

There is no one else who knows
what you know the way you know it
or who can express the unknown
in the way you can express it.

~ A Course of Love
D: Day 22.10

I know you might be slightly wary of this chapter, considering the title. In my blog publication of the story, an image of Cartman from the show *South Park* comically introduced the tale. I know...it doesn't sound all too spiritual, but hopefully, you'll discover otherwise.

One weekend, several years ago, a group of us took part in a retreat entitled Advanced Spiritual Healing. The weekend's experiences and opportunities – powerful heart-centered immersion in the Presence – resulted in abounding gratitude as we practiced many previously learned concepts: spiritual truths and messages relived in real-time and profoundly felt. First and foremost, this included the urgency of being a healer. Not that the group didn't already understand the importance of such impactful work, it's just that palpable urgency blared like an undimmable beacon, shaking us to our core. This profound shift, a change in our consciousness, was felt and repeatedly articulated as it rested in the retreat's reverberating subtext: We must be the light and step out of the closet to do it – not tomorrow, not next month or next year. *NOW. [Gulp!]*

Like many healers, staying in our comfort zone and only offering our "talents" cautiously – careful tiptoeing energy to avoid anticipated negative interactions – rang true as one causative agent of our hiding. Fear of our power, fear of failure, and mistrust in our intuition joined the long list of limiting beliefs that continued to keep us shrouded in secrecy. Common worries among those working with the unseen. However, the gentle but powerful wake of my "personal" healing[45] simply washed away these struggles and left an indelible mark. Here's what happened…

It's been two days of discussion and hands on spiritual healing. After participating in all of them, I finally feel drawn to be on the healing table for my own receiving. So, I lie down while others cover me with warm, comfortable blankets. Skilled healers, trusted companions encircle the

---

[45] Healing is a collective movement whereby the giver and receiver share transformation, perfectly and wholly. The idea of personal healing is known more to the personality. Our Spirit-self knows our connection to all of Life and life, facilitating healing that radiates out, shared by all.

table – people in the flesh, angels, guides, and passed over loved ones. The energy is strong but light and peaceful, and I feel fully immersed in loving God-energy.

Surrendering to the healing, I see a familiar image which enters my mind's eye – Yeshua Ben Joseph[46], otherwise known as the Master Jesus. He faces me, pleasant and welcoming, while standing confidently, dressed in white robes, reddish hair, and a smile. His arm casually fans over two blue-and-white plaid aluminum lawn chairs to offer me a seat, a lighthearted presentation that reminds me of Vanna White.[47] Handing me a red-and-white striped bin of popcorn, he asks me to "watch it all."

Filled with excitement and anticipation, like a child waiting for July 4th fireworks, I take the nearest chair, ready for an impressive show, one that's currently a mystery. Then, all at once, I can see the whole of Mother Earth spinning in Her blue-green glory; to the right is a massage table surrounded by healers, a healing in progress. I know, with palpable certainty, that Yeshua wants me to join him in "watching the illusions of life"...*all* of them. That is to say, the obvious ones that come with living in the physical realm and the more obscure ones, like those with healing.

Joining with him in observation, I hear, "When life makes you sad, remember this." Suddenly, a rush of joy and humor accompanies his words, so potent it makes me laugh out loud. This has never happened throughout

---

[46] Yeshua, a constant source of guidance, love, and assistance from the higher realms, available to all, was one of several teachers channeled through Rev. Penny Donovan. As a result, his energetic presence became quite familiar to me and many others.

[47] Vanna White is an American television personality and film actress known as the hostess of Wheel of Fortune since 1982.

many received healings, let alone with profound bliss-filled waves that burst through in deep-belly jiggling. The way Yeshua presented it all – the viewpoint, the chairs, the popcorn, his jubilant demeanor, and the healing energy – birthed this comedy. So, I succumb to a spontaneous fit of the giggles – I can't help myself – while other blockages linked to sadness disintegrate into nothingness.

It's been days since the retreat. Still, I question whether I fully understood the message. I am clear on our earthy illusions – the errors in our thinking that leave us feeling lesser-than, angry, sad, put upon, etc. But the concept of healings being an illusion has me rethinking my experience, especially on a weekend dedicated to the task. Yet, something about the depth and scope of Yeshua's message struck at my core, and I can't escape this gut-level wisdom.

Like many retreats, the Truth hiding behind our long-standing perceptions grows in potency as the remnants of our old beliefs fall away. It's kind of like stripping furniture; the beauty of the underlying wood appears as we clear away layers of old paint or varnish. For me, a deeper understanding of material life's mirages profoundly integrated into my heart, vibrating with every cell and well into realms beyond the body. With it came a surrender of archaic paradigms, to *know* healing – an experience meant to remove any blockages to the sacred Truth that lies within us – as illusion. Why? Because Source created us in His/Her/Its image. Perfect. Loved. Lovable and whole. How could perfection need healing?

Then again, how do we get "there," the place of knowing our perfection? It's a journey, a winding trail, because we've long believed in unworthiness and separation from the Divine. Thankfully, however, releasing the thoughts and feelings that do not serve us uncovers a memory, an Essence so sacred and holy that words fall short. And because our grace-filled and divine Self remains, ever untouched, It continues to guide us Homeward, bringing forth the Creator's vision of us as perfect Children.

In summary, I can say this:

Everything about this world is illusionary. A "dream within a dream." (Shakespeare had it right.) That doesn't mean we aren't experiencing what happens in our lives or that it's not real to us. However, it has no true substance, no impact on our eternalness. And when we can see our world as impermanent and understand how the physical realm's debacles and many events are meaningless to our forever Self, we can rest in the Divine truth that...

> Only Love and what we
> uncover through Love is real.

Now, I can hear you say, "But that horrible thing happened, and I can touch that...see that!"

Yes, you can...and life does happen. This is the five-sense game of ego that wants us to only believe in the reverse order of the Universe, the physical over Spirit. Always the physical. But that thinking is backward, the upside-down mindset of personality, trying to keep our consciousness here, instead of knowing...

Only the Divine is real.

By infinite, loving grace, the action-energy of Source will use our misperceptions, illnesses, and difficulties, turning them into powerful learning opportunities (really unlearning). And as we move past what appears to be a corporeal hell, witnessing and cultivating a sense of higher meaning helps us grow, to see life and healing differently.

All healing, regardless of the difficulty, is our awakening to Source within us, through the God-self of us. There is the Divine and us. Truly, there is only the Divine...

Source experiencing life in many, many forms.

As we surrender the layers of illusionary beliefs about our body, in our emotions, and of our lower mind, we awaken. The crystals, candles, and even the laying on of hands are props. Any healing "tool" is a way we facilitate our connection to Source, aiding us to be One in the same Holy energy, an energy that travels to exactly where It's needed.

The wound is the place where the Light enters.

~ Rumi

Our recognition of Source within ourselves and others – the Christ love of our very core, unconditional and compassionate – is the spark that lights the flame, a portal upward into the light.

What "needs to be healed" is only real to us because *we* created it, not Source. And only we can liberate ourselves from these barriers to Awareness, to the Divine, through willingness and by allowing the action of God to work through us.

As our made-up aspects fall away in the luminous water-fall of Sacred energy, our inner light shines. Moreover, we will only "need" healing (*believe* we need healing) until *we know who we are* – beauty incarnate, pure, whole, and loving in our Truth.

So, whenever the world gets crazy, life gets heavy, or you just need a break from the madness, join Yeshua and me with a lawn chair and some popcorn, and remember...

'dis gon b'gud.'

To life! To your adventure! To loving yourself and this wild ride!

Reflections

❀ *What are your feelings and thoughts about this chapter?*

❀ *Have you been open to receive healing in a multitude of forms?*

❀ *What are the beliefs you hold that could be stopping you from living life to the fullest? Are you ready to change them?*

❀ *How do you think Source sees you? If there is negativity in that thought, how might you change it?*

Over the Rainbow

Someday I'll wish upon a star and
Wake up where the clouds are far behind me.
Where trouble melts like lemon drops
High above the chimney tops
That's where you'll find me.
~ Arlen & Harburg.
The Wizard of Oz

As I was in this book's final edits, another chapter serendipitously unfolded (something that's happened more than once). It's a bittersweet story about the gifts from our precious fluffernutter Ash Mayard Nicastro.

Ash, an amazing pup, came to us – as I described before in *Tiny Toes* – on the heels of a challenging divorce. He is undeniably cute in a living-stuffed-animal kind of way, a white, fluffy Muppet teddy bear with pale beige spots. So many, especially children, just had to pet him, drawn to his utter fluffernutiness.

As I grew in my spiritual practice, a whole other kind of relationship with Ash developed. Never did that become more evident than when he began to travel to spiritual retreats with Sacred Garden Fellowship.

You see, as a Lhasa Apso, Ash is a natural meditator. Originating from the Tibetan mountains, monks and royalty historically employed his breed to guard the inside walls of monasteries, temples, and palaces. So, the energy of meditation and sacred gatherings flows through him, ribbons of peaceful groundedness woven into DNA and spiritual essence. And his canine howls... actually, high-pitched oms.

At retreats, Ash would make his rounds between sessions and on breaks, visiting some and greeting all who said hello. But during the teachings and meditation, he was a quiet, stoic presence (minus his occasional sneezing, coughing, panting, or times being tempted by our evening desserts that waited on a table for the group; he is still a dog, you know).

Over time, Ash became a mascot of sorts for our spiritual group. A welcome participant and fellow healer.

Yes, I said healer.

I can almost hear the questions forming in your brain (or maybe that's a projection of what I think you're thinking). Nevertheless, Ash is a healer, one with a unique methodology, one characteristically doggish. You see, Ash offered his healing through canine expressiveness. In other words, he healed as a discriminating (picky, even) humper. Sometimes there seemed to be no rhyme or reason to his choices, but he knew exactly what he was doing. Only years later, did his purpose become clear.

Now I know how this sounds. And perhaps you're even thinking, "Seriously? How could doggie humping be healing?"

First, take your dirty little brain out of the gutter for a moment and consider this: we all have innate abilities, and yes, humping for a dog is associated with sexual behavior. That said, ask yourself: why do dogs have sex? Is it not a manifestation of their creative nature?

You see, human avenues of creation are broader, inclusive of things like art, music, architecture, and cooking, to name a few. But creativity on a purely physical level, a common thread among all creatures, is to bring life into the world after their own kind. (Dogs make dogs. Tulips make tulips, etc.) So, sex, sublimated to an energy, is creativity expressed, causing God to become more manifest in the corporeal realm. Sexual sparks arise from that innate desire to become more, to be One, the Divine flow of the Father/Mother through the channel of sex. Ash merely used his creative energy in alignment with being a dog through canine sexual behavior. Simply put, he gave healing through humping. (*Stop snickering.*)

Ash's desire to help sometimes came as an "of course," especially with people recovering from a known illness like that of our friend and fellow healer on the mend from surgery. But at other times, he surprised us all, tuning into something not yet outwardly manifested. His instinct never became more apparent than during a workshop with one of my regular students, Becky.

As soon as Becky sat down for the afternoon class, Ash made a beeline for her leg, panting all the way. Humorously surprised but quite familiar with Ash, Becky just shrugged off his approach, denying any illness or struggles, even when I explained that he sensed her need for healing. Perhaps uncanny or even inconceivable, Ash never approached Becky like that during all their previous encounters. However, several times that day, I pulled Ash from Becky like lint off Velcro while she vehemently affirmed her health. Affirmed, that is, until a few mornings later when I received this email...

Good morning Adriene,

I just wanted to let you know how incredibly right your dog was on Tuesday about me needing healing. Since I was feeling perfectly fine, I was sure he was just picking up on the negative energy I dragged with me from the bad day at my house. I did not know yet that I was about to have a major episode with diverticulosis... I manage that condition really well by avoiding high fat and processed foods, but I've been recently indulging in too much of my favorite summertime treats, like French fries, ice cream, and frozen cheesecake on a stick. I woke up at 2 a.m. Wednesday morning feeling really sick, and by 4 a.m. the evacuation of everything in my digestive system began. I spent much of yesterday in the bathroom completing that process, and I am still not well today. Yesterday, while hugging the toilet too many times, I kept thinking how I wish I would have allowed your little guy to just hump my leg all night!!

Just want you to know that I am in complete awe of your dog. His intuition is amazing. I had no idea how sick I was going to be in just hours after seeing him Tuesday night. What an amazing dog!

~ Becky

We feel the same, Becky. And in the process of obtaining Becky's permission to include her experience in this chapter, she reminded me of her diagnosis from that episode in 2016 – severe gastroenteritis. She was sick for a week but took nearly three to recover. How we should have listened to the great, white fluffernutter!

Ash has been a healing companion for years, but after downsizing and moving out of our long-time home (25 years, in fact) in 2019, he and Zannah became permanent fixtures in my new treatment room. Sometimes he will offer his humping magic, but mostly he holds a reassuring and grounding presence. With my younger clients and the more anxious ones, he's a happy, tongue-wagging, whiskery friend.

We thought severe illness with Lyme, just following our move, would take him from us, but somehow, he pulled through. Not without complications, however.

Soon to be fourteen in April 2021, Ash struggles with arthritis, dementia, and the lingering effects of Lyme. The boys and I talk several times about Ash's decline. It seems like a waiting game, considering his age. No one can anticipate what may come.

For three weeks now, Ash roams the floors at night, a ghost wandering aimlessly in the dark. I hear him panting heavily, claws click-clacking on the oak hardwood.

Deep in this January coldness of 2021, several nights deliver more unsettled energy. I open my eyes countless times, awakened by a kind of tick – Ash's feet shuffling in even rhythm, front left to front right and back again. He reminds me of a soldier in static formation, knees repeatedly lifted to the sky but going nowhere.

At 2:00 a.m. his silhouette graces the doorway of my bedroom again, marked by audible clicking. I can hear it from where I lie, despite the air filter's blaring white noise. After a few more hours of sleep, I awaken again at 6:15 a.m. Ash stands in the same spot, marching... always marching and staring into the room as dawn streams into the space. *Didn't he move at all?* Something is disquieting about his time-frozen stance, and I know without a doubt that his dementia has grown considerably.[48]

Days and sometimes nights become marked with a sense of burden and difficulty. After weeks of broken and absent sleep, I try to remain calm with him but feel exasperated and attempt to correct the uncorrectable – the pacing-peeing-scratching-barking madness.

---

[48] Though officially diagnosed with dementia in 2019, Ash began to show signs in 2013.

Guilt starts to fill the space left behind by my frustration, so I make amends with him and work to cultivate more patience. Always, patience.

It's February, and other new symptoms – insatiable thirst – add to an already long list. Drinking a whole bowl of water matches Ash's constant peeing. Frequently, I awaken to urine puddles the size of a small lake. During the day, sometimes he makes it to the bathroom, other times not. Even doggie diapers can't contain the volume that his kidneys won't process.

A trip to the vet yields few conclusions. He doesn't have diabetes but could be having some kidney issues. Regardless, his bloodwork is unremarkable. Old age may be the biggest culprit.

Client sessions are a whole other challenge now. Ash's previously quiet and supportive energy changes to anxiousness and confusion – a daytime cocktail of discomfort and dementia – making a once predictable animal a hotbed of chaos. Only now do I *almost* miss the weeks of January sundowning. At least he slept while I worked.

It's March and another visible shift surfaces. After weeks of confusion and accidents, what I once saw as anxiety has changed to terror – a frantic attempt to outrun the inescapable. He jolts from states of relaxed sleep, dashing across the floor with such speed that it startles me. Today it happened repeatedly, and somehow, what seems like a random event has become cemented in my awareness as a desperate need to escape pain.

This morning it's clear that he cannot find comfort alone and follows me everywhere. In the kitchen I take a step, and so does he. If I sit, he wants to be on my lap – uncharacteristic behavior for this furry four-footed. As today's sessions begin, he stands chair-side, scratching my leg. When I look down, all I see are pleading eyes. They scream a panicked subtext: *Get me out of here!* Literally. So, on my lap is where I take him, a place he strangely and not so strangely welcomes. Thankfully, he finds some comfort in the closeness and sleeps.

Now, all my client's sessions happen with Ash either next to me or on my lap. Regardless, he wakes in the same fitful starts, darting from resting states to run across the room or jumping from the chair to dodge his discomfort.

One thing has become evident...his time is close. The dreaded realization arrives without doubt as I watch pain become this dog's master. Even his bowels abandon him. *Where is the dignity and peace in that?* Thankfully, toddler diapers help prevent house floods, but that doesn't stop the unexpected poop emergencies – not making it to the door on time or even forgetting where the door is.

It's March 16, 2021, and I prep for a visit with Finn over six hours away. The pet sitter is ready for convalescent care, so I schedule a routine COVID test to comply with college visitor status, one requested by Finn.

Something else presses on me, though. To leave Ash behind with such discomfort is unsettling, so I call the vet for pain meds to make his weekend more bearable. Worse, I must tell the boys...the dreaded conversation we've been bracing for.

Later that evening, I take to the phone. But first, I swallow the lump in my throat that accompanies a palpable ache of sadness and try to find the words.

"It's close, guys. He's in a lot of pain, and I don't think it's fair to keep him burdened if this continues."

We cry together, and the boys talk to him on speaker, preparing for the inevitable. The sadness of seeing him go blends with knowing it's the kindest option. Even though our agreement is unanimous, it doesn't make the choice any easier, a decision with unclear timing.

Wednesday, March 17. Packing, prepping, clients, and Ash care. These are the tasks before me.

Folding jeans and light sweaters into my green rolling suitcase, I consider the upcoming weekend, hoping that the pet sitter won't be too overwhelmed.

If I test positive for COVID, this packing is all for nothing, I think.

Where's that thought from?

Probably just anticipatory fear.

❖

It's Thursday, March 18. The sun is bright and lights the whole bedroom, making any return to sleep doubtful. I pick up my phone to check early morning email, scanning for cancelations and other important notices. Today is my last day to finalize packing, so I multitask, making a mental list of clothes to collect while scrolling through my inbox.

Hmmm…COVID results. Good timing, since I leave tomorrow.

Positive! What?!

I stare at the screen…*almost* in shock. Forget anticipatory fear; intuition tried to warn me.

I have COVID… [Sigh. Slight nervousness.]

I have COVID! Oh my God, I can sleep!

Oh boy. Look at that.

Two distinctly different reactions flood my awareness. First, mild anxiety with having COVID combines with heavy disappointment that I can't see my son. And second, undeniable relief.

Rest only in the event of sickness – this should not be the case – but that's my blockage, needing an excuse for time off. Well…I have it now.

Largely asymptomatic except for lingering asthma symptoms and a headache, I take the day to rest and wait for the vet to return my call. Even though I'm not traveling, pain medication still seems like a helpful intervention.

In the meantime, if Ash can sit with me on the couch, resting, he's relatively calm. Thankfully, we're stocked with groceries, clean laundry, and a sufficiently tidy house. The powers-that-be created a divinely orchestrated quarantine; luckily, I seem to have enough energy to take care of myself and the animals.

Life – now relegated to binge-watching, reading, journaling, drawing, and generally laying low – feels strange. But too much activity causes my headache to surge, so I'm forced to be still – a state that I've frequently challenged.

On a higher level, I stay present to what's before me and routinely send Ash healing, wrapping him in love-light for his highest good. Tonight, connected in that sacred flow, I sense another presence near him. With third-eye vision, I catch the gentle astral hand of Rev. Penny stroking the hair on Ash's back as he sleeps. The healing touch of my beloved teacher brings more tears to already weepy eyes, knowing we have so much help from the other side.

Tuesday, March 23, I pick up Ash's pain medication. After one pill, he is doing his glorious butt-twerking happy dance, moving with freedom and ease. It's wonderful to see him comfortable and enjoying life, frolicking like the Ash we know. On the other hand, though, guilt sneaks into my mindscape. *Why didn't I call sooner? Could he have had more pain-free days?*

❖

Thursday, March 25. I have an answer to my silent question. A resounding, NO! He is restless, moving about the bed – spinning, scooting, and repeatedly panting heavily. By 4:00 a.m. I help him to the floor, and he wanders the house well into Friday's morning hours. When I finally rise nearing 8:00 a.m., I find him still pacing, but that's not all. Other evidence of the medicine's side-effects – vomit. It's everywhere throughout the first floor, six piles to be exact.

All Friday, Ash's system cannot process water, let alone food, and every bit of liquid he drinks comes back up. His breathing is rapid and shallow, mixed with segments of heavy panting. When he stands to go out or drink, his legs won't hold him long enough to pee or lap water. (I suspect a kidney condition, looming in the background, exacerbated by his pain medicine – the toxic capsule that created a terrible turn.)

So, I hold the bowl close to him as he lays in the kitchen, hoping it eases his difficulties, and we count on new toddler diapers to fix the other. At times he tries to drink on his own but mostly refuses water, and his weakness grows. Trying to keep him hydrated, I offer a dropper-full of water and electrolyte-loaded fluids every half hour, praying that it begins to rebalance his system and helps him regain strength. Normally, it just dribbles out of his mouth. Either he can't or won't swallow.

I am overwhelmed by warring parts of myself: one feels pressure to take him to the emergency vet, while another believes it will render nothing but more discomfort – medical extremes in a sterile and chaotic environment. I lost faith in mainstream veterinary treatment long ago –

its conventionality, chemically dependent interventions, and unwholesome allopathic drive – but more so, now, with his recent drug-induced spiral. So, I must balance my skepticism and caution with the desire to honor Ash and his aging body. Today, the need to maintain this precarious equilibrium by staying home outweighs seeking someone in a white lab coat. Moreover, I feel guilty for giving him the prescribed medicine, wishing I had thought of CBD oil or another alternative.

Worry and fear cycle through every conscious thought, until finally, I surrender to a higher knowing that draws me to contemplative meditation. In this consciousness, a heartfelt connection with Ash offers information: he wants to stay home...with his furry siblings and me. Still, I don't trust the message, more so my ability to clearly receive from him. *Are imagination and personality feeding me what I want to hear?*

Thankfully, Spirit always provides the perfect opportunities for healing and growth. (Yes, I know you've read this many times.) As such, I have a call with a friend and colleague. The conversation could not be timelier.

Explaining my struggles with Ash, she shares her thoughts and then connects me with Shari, an animal communicator. I hope the answers I seek will come, desired help to me ease his comfort and honor his last wishes.

Saturday, March 27. Shari kindly agrees to my urgent request for pet communication[49] with Ash. Most pressing is his health and knowing how to assist him. The wondering, guessing, and heavy grief feel like blocks, clouded-over knowingness to blanket my avenue of good guidance. Shari's help feels divinely arranged.

Session for Ash Mayard Nicastro[50]
Date: 3/27/21 Time: 7:50 am – 8:18 am.

Willing to Talk? – "Yes, of course. I've been waiting to talk." (Very sweet, stoic dog...hides his discomfort. Adores his family. Very polite...he kept calling me Ma'am.)

Do you have a job here? "I'm the official greeter for the family. I check everyone out to see if they are okay."

How are you feeling?

Emotionally: "I'm pretty content...I can feel the worry that surrounds me, but I know everything will be okay." **What do you mean by okay?** "All will go as God's plan." (Very strong spiritual connection.)

Physically: "Oh, my little body feels full...my insides feel too big for my outsides."

Do you have any pain or discomfort anywhere? "A general fullness...it gives me pain in my back. Breathing is a bit strained like my lungs can't fill up as much. I try

---

[49] Animals can communicate with humans via telepathic messages. This occurs whereby the person communicating must match their vibration with the animal to give and receive information.

[50] Session via Shari Koval, SKenergyhealing.com.

to take deeper breaths, but they end up being shallow and panting. It's hard to find a comfortable place to settle."

What can your family do to make your life better? "Cool and soft areas feel the best." (To rest.)

Do you have any funny habits that you wish to share? "I used to walk around on my hind legs when I was younger...like a circus dog."

Specific messages / questions:

1. Do you want to leave the earth plane? "I feel my time is close. My Soul wants to soar and explore but it is 'caged' inside my failing body. I'm ready when the time comes."

2. When it is time, do you want mom to help you by taking you to the vet and use medicine to leave or would you rather stay with her and pass on your own? "I'd love to be held by Mom during the transition, but I don't know if I will go on my own. I may need some help."

Will you give your Mom a sign to know you need help to go? "I will be laying on my side and lift my head to hold eye contact. I will hold it for a long time, then blink and sigh. Mom will know."

3. Do you think you'll be able to make it until next weekend for Finn to come home from college and visit with you? "I'm really going to try. Finn is such a good friend to me. If my body needs to go sooner, I'd like to hear his voice before I go."

4. Where is your pain? "My whole belly is painful and tender. It just feels so full and it causes pain in my back and hips."

5. Is the CBD oil Mom gave you after you threw up so many times helping with pain or feeling sick in the belly? "It kind of dulls it a bit. It does help me to be able to relax a bit more."

6. Do you know what made you get sick and throw up so many times Friday? "There was just no more room in my belly. Small amounts of liquids I can tolerate. I don't feel all that hungry right now, but anything I took in just came back out. I was trying to empty space in my belly...to relieve the pressure."

7. Is there anywhere else you feel bad? "Not really...I just need a whole new inside." (He smiles.)

8. Do you remember what other lifetimes you've been in together? "I can't really remember any specifics but the first time I saw you this time, I knew I was home. You feel like home to me. We have our own unspoken language. You know me better than anyone. You see me and you hear me."

9. Will you come back to the earth plane again? "I want to observe from above for a while. I think I've completed my 'task list' of things to teach and learn. I'll always be connected with you...you will feel me and hear me... especially when you are driving."

10. Is there anything else you'd like to tell Mom? "Oh, the lives you have changed for the better. I am in awe of you. Thank you for discussing your plans with me and letting me be a sounding board for new ideas. We are two halves of a greater whole. I won't leave you when I go...I'll just give you a 'higher' point of view."

12. Is there something Mom could do that would make you happy? "Let's sit outside more and listen to nature.

Let's sit in the grass and follow my nose for a while. Let's not worry about what's to come...let's just be."

13. What more can Mom do to help? "Gently rub my spine...the muscles get so tight there. Talk about my upcoming journey with joy...just love me."

Messages for your family: "I've had a wonderful time here. Thank you for letting me be a part of every moment. I loved to supervise everything. I know you will all be okay...just keep looking forward and look up for advice."

I feel so grateful and blessed by this communication – its depth, clarity, and the peace of mind it brought. What I did not expect were such loving and beautiful personal messages from Ash. His affirmations of the work I do, how he feels with/about us. Our grace-filled connections warm my heart.

Still, tears of joy mix with the sadness of Ash's decline. In this moment, it feels like too much. Too much, but this is my journey with him. At least I know how he will communicate his last wishes, telling me when he's ready to leave. For now, though, it seems unimaginable; he can't even lift his head, and I must transport him everywhere, a heavy rag draped over my arms. His desire to hear of what's to come – his moving on and travels "over the rainbow" in happy tones – is my only way to cultivate a sense of peace.

"It won't be long now, buddy. You'll see all your fur friends. Bu, Levi, Buddy, Nala, Daisy, Lincoln...they'll be there to greet you." Grief-tightened throat muscles try to strangle the words, but I refuse to stop, reminding him of all those that went before him, those expecting him when he makes his final leap. "Everyone is waiting for you, sweetie...Penny, Virgil, Suzanne...even Yeshua will be there for you."

Heartache sucks all air from the room, my lungs, my cells. Like a black hole, it leaves a vacuous void blown through my insides, threatening to consume me. Ash's coming transition marks the end of an era, one punctuated with such force that I must stop and remain mindful to its gifts. He's been part of our lives for so long, and I feel as if I've taken him for granted, like the Sun.

Instead, I try to rest in his presence – a grounding and stabilizing force no matter how chaotic – to cherish the moments, now. Unflappable, stoic, and dependable, his loyalty and steadfastness will always be with us. This, I trust.

It's curious to witness the profound impact and energy of another, how it becomes so palpable upon the threat of their absence. Take away one furry, four-footed protector from his earthly home, and the result is a certain emptiness. So, I choose to shift my vision of the pup that lies before me; this is *not* the dog I know. Instead, for brief snapshots in time, I remember his soft eyes, bright demeanor, prancy-pants gate, and bubble-gum pink smile. I let *this* fill the void. And it does, until my heart is crushed by other moments – one hurricane-size gust that sucks every molecule of air out of the room, yet again. The gut-punch loss hits my solar plexus with an invisible squashing fist, and I am bent in half, hollow.

As Saturday wears on, the weight of Ash's decline sits in the center of my world, and I do all I can to ease his discomfort. Every activity is reduced to the utmost simplicity, and we become the home of bodily functions and intense emotions. Thankfully, I have several friends who support me along the way. Their kind words and practical guidance are the strong arms that hold me. My faith in Source, the angels, and all help beyond the veil is a soothing balm for worn nerves and a hurting heart.

Sunday morning, March 28. He's drinking on his own!

In one sudden burst of energy, Ash stands and takes a drink of water on his own. I'm not sure what this means but remain hopeful.

As the day wears on, he drinks a bit more, but he's a shell of himself. Still, there's happiness and relief for such simple things.

Thankfully, sleep fills the day for all of us. Ash sleeps the most, as he's done in the past 48 hours; so much sleep, as if he's already halfway Home, while I cycle the ups and downs of grief, hope, and uncertainty. Fortunately, continued catch-ups with friends keep me sane. One such heartfelt call with Katrina brings many insights.

Just to preface, I need to say that a profound gift of consciously being on a spiritual path – actively listening to our Higher Self – is that answers and awareness are available, instantly. They always are, but practiced connection makes us attuned to the guidance.

On the call with Katrina, I discussed my hesitation with taking Ash to the emergency vet, wondering in one of those out-loud streams of consciousness, "the reason behind my visceral resistance." Instantly, I know – a string of associations that connect emergency care with death...

the death of one tiny infant from the past life of my Puritan teen-self, the threat of "outsiders," the mercy and pain of helping a loved one release the body. (See *Making Lemonade.*) It is an awareness challenging to describe but deeply felt. No words can adequately capture what surfaces from my inner depths.

As we continue to talk, I receive a message, one from a healing for Ash and our family. In summary, it's my inner child that deeply mourns his loss and he, in turn, is hanging on to protect her.

Katrina's grace-filled words lead me to a contemplative meditation. In this space, I join Spirit to Spirit with my inner child and Ash, inviting him to meet me in the higher planes while connecting with that part of me who could keep Ash unnecessarily tethered to his body and earth life. At first, an image emerges: my young toddler-self holding Alfie – a sweet Maltese, close in appearance to Ash. Memories of Alfie flood my consciousness, and I remember how he just "disappeared" one day, a suspicious event seemingly linked to the irritation he caused my then father. Now, I meet the remnants of that loss, the sadness and confusion of never getting to say goodbye.

The memory of Alfie comes and goes quickly, segueing to another: Ace, a beautiful golden and black German Shepherd. Ace was my first guardian and protector, so clever that he could open doors with his mouth. I see the image of his long snout carefully positioned on the old brass knob of our heavy kitchen door. Then, the vision shifts to show our outside play, limited to the front yard; here, I watch him gently pull the collar of my t-shirt, helping right my tiny body. He was the perfect mix of intellectual sharpness and tender touch.

I can acutely feel Ace's protective energy and the serendipitous way it aligns with Ash. It's as if they are the same dog, Ash having returned to finish a job cut short by an abusive father. The awareness, clear and calming, speaks to a contract, one made and finally fulfilled.

Turning my attention back to my inner toddler, she sits in my mind's eye quietly on my lap. I watch her extend a chubby little hand, palm up to Ash. His fluffy white whiskers brush against her pink skin as he licks her fingertips.

"I have her now, buddy. I promise to take care of her...to protect her."

"You're done your job...so beautifully. Thank you, Ash. Thank you, old friend. It's okay to go Home. We'll be okay."

I let the tears of grief, gratitude, and healing flow in well-worn paths across my pale cheeks while keeping a hand on Ash's back, pausing between long soft strokes to help ease his discomfort. His transition is closer than ever, a certainty that has no words, only a profound and abiding feeling.

I silently hope he gives me the signs he told Shari, but I must act mercifully and help him leave tomorrow if he doesn't. It's only fair.

It's late, now, well past the witching hour. Try as I might to find rest, I cannot help but check on Ash repeatedly, like a mother who checks on a sick child. My hand rests on his back or hip, whatever is closer, a soft touch to let him know he has company, a connection to ease my sense of worry and abiding grief.

Every few hours he resumes his escape, belly-crawling around the bed to outmaneuver pain and discomfort. So, I repeat the CBD oil which has been helping him settle after the medication failed. Gently sneaking it under his tongue, I can smell the funny earthy tones lingering on his breath. They bring a certain comfort, reminding me that he's still here.

Monday, March 29. The light streams in the window, casting pinkish shadows across my bedroom's pale blue walls and cream dresser. Ash is stirring, so I offer him a drink of water in a cut-off yogurt container – a shallow makeshift bowl easier for his tongue to navigate. He willingly takes in the coolness and lies down facing me. As I pet his head, he looks at me, blinking in a way that speaks of presence. It's the most conscious he's been for days, and so we lie among the messy covers staring at one another. Connected in a place beyond the need for words, he stares, seconds bleeding into minutes. I stare back, suspended in timelessness. Then, he blinks one last time, before holding his head up momentarily. A loud, unmistakable sigh escapes his throat.

Oh my God, he did it. This is the answer to my question, the exchange I thought would never happen, especially from a dog too sick to lift his head. But today, he is present and intent on letting me know. *He's ready.* A sense of peace fills the space once occupied by intense sadness.

Taking to the phone, I begin my call chain, searching for other vets. Wanting to take him to a small office instead of some big slick clinic, I fail at attempts to find an opening. Regardless, the understanding is clear: reservations about a large facility are my blockage. *He's ready to go Home. Any place will do.* So, I call his vet, making an appointment for the "comfort room" at 11:30 a.m. We have a few short hours to say our final goodbyes.

A text from my oldest son Kaleb makes the day's scheduled tasks all too real. After explaining the turn of events, events discussed more times than I can count, Kaleb decides to video conference and say goodbye, too. Time and distance prevents him from being here, but in truth, seeing Ash in person would be just too painful. Remembering him healthy, especially for a psychic kiddo like Kaleb, is far more necessary. As for Finn, he's away at championships. Fearful of derailing months of intense work, Kaleb and I decide to leave Finn's earlier goodbye in the same company as Kaleb's long-distance call, a difficult decision, too, but one that feels necessary.

I think you can gather what happened next. I'll spare you the details, but I will say this. When Ash's heart stopped, he popped out of his body with unmistakable exuberance. His unbridled joy, the freedom from pain and an old body, matched a vision from Katrina – Ash leaping with joy over rainbows. And what do you know... synchronicity strikes again. Nearly three weeks ago, I put rainbows on my phone's wallpaper with the following lyrics by George Matheson...

> Oh, joy that seeketh me through pain,
> I cannot close my heart to thee,
> I trace the rainbow through the rain,
> And feel the promise is not vain
> That morn shall tearless be.

The weeks following Ash's transition are almost tearless. *Almost.* Grief comes in waves – sometimes on silent cat feet, sometimes like torrential rain. This exquisite pain, born of profound love, is a love I fear as lost. Still, grief truly makes me feel the depth and breadth of love's presence, and remember, yet again, that we never lose anything as eternal as love.

Gratitude genuinely fills my heart, the gift of Ash's lifetime – nearly fourteen years of precious memories, sacred moments in his passing, beautiful support from the other side. Spirit provided two heart-warming weeks (with COVID) to be with him, to care for him and recover missing pieces of old loss. As painful as it has been, I wouldn't trade it for the world. It's just a part of what we do for our furry, four-footed children, who give us so much.

Here's to you, Ash! For teaching me patience, reminding me to live with joy, helping me rest and be present, for your unending loyalty and steadfastness, enduring protection and grounding, your healing heart and loving touch.

I love you. We love you. You'll be forever in our hearts.

❖

Reflections

❖ *Have you experienced the loss of someone special in your life? How has it affected you?*

❖ *Can you witness the gifts offered by that someone?*

❖ *How might you honor any remaining feelings of loss?*

❖ *How might you celebrate all that someone brought to enrich your life?*

Ash Mayard Nicastro
April 2008 – March 2021

Redemption Song

In the midst of hate. I found there was.
within me. an invincible love. In the midst of tears.
I found there was. within me. an invincible smile.
In the midst of chaos. I found there was. within me. an
invincible calm. I realized. through it all. that…
In the midst of winter. I found there was. within me. an
invincible summer. And that makes me happy.
For it says that no matter how hard the world pushes
against me. within me. there's something stronger –
something better. pushing right back.
~Albert Camus

It's been the strangest of times. Most likely, I don't need to tell you that. If, however, you're reading this long past 2021, then perhaps you heard stories about the pandemic of 2019 from a friend or relative. Whatever the case, weirdness has become the new normal.

For me, all these months of quarantine and racial tension brought forth stubborn error perceptions that I've carried for lifetimes. The theme? Redemption...but not the kind of redemption most think of, as in:

Redemption [rə'dem(p)SH(ə)n] – the action of saving or being saved from sin, error, or evil; the action of regaining or gaining possession of something in exchange for payment, or clearing a debt.

Let me just say this: I did not need saving from sin because I don't believe in that. (That's not to say that unloving acts don't exist or that I'm incapable of them. I just see sin as the ego in action, the choice of fear over love, but that's a conversation for another day.) My redemption was all about me. That is, redemption from myself, for...

I have seen the enemy, and the enemy is me.[51]

As for "paying a price," I did, indeed. Not through a traditional exchange of monies or sacrifice in a physical sense but a "cost" nonetheless. The metaphorical coins of my payment – personal fear, perceived loss, belief in lack, and attachments to the earth plane – tainted gold minted in old treasures that didn't serve me. I paid my dues by letting them all go, even though they looked sparkly and enticing enough to keep while the world felt menacing.

My transformative journey – to leave behind ego, reclaim the Truth in me, actively remember my connection to

---

[51] A pun based on the famous quotation "We have met the enemy, and they are ours" – one of two famous quotes made by American Navy Commodore Oliver Hazard Perry on September 10, 1813, after defeating a British naval squadron on Lake Erie during the War of 1812.

Source, and know that only I can change my world, my personal world – crossed many months, leaving indelible marks on my soul. It started like this…

❖

It's February 23, 2020, and one day seems to bleed into the next, typical bookends to the weeks disappearing. Time has become a hazy ghost, mocking me; the more I reach for it, the emptier it feels and the wispier I seem.

Yet again, I search for something to occupy another night in isolation. *Damn those disappearing bookends.*

News of COVID-19 continues to spread like a brushfire burning out of control, the kind one watches from a distance thinking that no amount of water or help will quell the blaze. Medical and government-driven interventions seem to falter across the globe, while the media creates an ongoing feeding frenzy; hungry human sharks desperately snap at all shreds of information. Some of it intelligent, most of it junk. Yet, while misinformation and socially-generated rumors spread, the science, statistics, and actual data remain a mystery. Who knows what's really going on? Only time will tell, so I serve up patience for breakfast, lunch, and dinner…and wait.

There's a path forming from living room to kitchen like a newly forged forest trail. This hike from sofa to fridge, fridge to sofa, is dangerously short. No calories burned on my travels; instead, they generate consumption and added pounds. A million snacks sit between traditionally timed meals. (Yes, I look forward to 8:00 a.m., 12:00 p.m., and 5:00 p.m. Call me Pavlov's dog.) Mostly, it's boredom and disconnect gnawing on my insides, not hunger. *The monsters need something sweet to keep them quiet.* Sadly, they win, but bags of black licorice only last so long. So, I begin to amuse myself, wondering if the oak floor-boards lining my path will darken or crack first. A running bet with empty bystanders – dining room chairs that silently tease me – say the odds seem stacked for dark and dirty. *God, I hope!*

It's March 4, 2020. The heavy weight of terror hangs in the air – a toxic gray mist thick enough to cut. The ethers, dripping with dread and panic, feel contaminated, like water polluted by pitch-black sludge. Though I can sense it all around me, one peek at the internet tells me I don't need to look far; many stories provide tangible evidence of what's resting in the unseen.

Added to my lingering concerns of the pandemic, this morning I can't breathe. An invisible elephant took up residence on my chest, ribs crushing under its wrinkly, gray weight, while my lungs wheeze in short, raspy expulsions, like an old coal furnace sputtering crusty smoke and ash.

Pained thoughts burn through hot neural pathways searching for answers to the death rattle. *My God, am I getting it? No fever, no chills, no sniffles…this is so weird!*

Where would I have gotten COVID? I've been around so few people, let alone anyone sick. And better yet, I don't even believe in contagion.[52]

I guess part of me, somewhere, still does.

---

[52] See *Glossary* regarding the metaphysical symbolism.

❖

Two days of rest, meditation, and gentle care yield inconsistent results. The gloomy pachyderm comes and goes with palpable reminders of its steadfast position. It ominously whispers to my lungs, "Forget breathing while I'm here."

Enough of this insanity! This energy needs to go! Frustration surges out of every cell in my body. Perhaps, it's just enough to force a change. However, another heaviness, born of disappointment and exasperation, adds to my gray enemy while my usual interventions to previous breathing issues collapse.

As hope begins to disappear along with my breath, bronchioles become stupefied, punch-drunk under this strange heaviness. *Clearly, something more insidious than an unhealed allergenic response is to blame.*

So I sit, open for inspiration and understanding, a pregnant pause that holds its breath. (No pun intended.) Somewhere between the heaviness and the Void awareness strikes – a tungsten lightbulb in a darkened room. *This weight and shortness of breath is not my energy! It's the mass consciousness of panic and illness that I absorbed. I can't believe that it manifested so physically!*

I've worn other people's energy before, but never this intensely. My own residual fear clearly built a landing pad, and I just called in the mother of all choppers. *Ugh!*

Taking the newfound awareness into meditation, I lift myself out of the weight and the accompanying feelings of death, tragic grief, and panic. Then, through auric surgery and cleansing, I remove the negative energy and replace it with peace and perfect health.

In the next few hours, a steady transformation occurs; I can breathe again. The elephant retreats to the jungle of chaos. Sanity restored. *Haaa-le-lu-jahhhhh!* A little tune erupts from rejoicing brain cells to accompany my tangible relief. I, however, walk a thin line between liberation and outright shock. So, gentleness with myself – a break for recovery and more space to ground realizations – is my prescription.

I've been teaching spiritual energy healing for years, working with energetic protection, and navigating the world as an empath, and *never* have I experienced this level of current psychic contamination. This "pollution," created by the dense mass consciousness, is an energy-sensitive's nightmare and so intense that it seemed surreal. Still, I cannot deny the change in how I feel emotionally and physically after cleaning the energy, meditating, and removing it from my aura, with the understanding that it didn't belong to me. As a well-behaved empath, I merely took it in like a raggedy, homeless animal...or a lost baby elephant who convinced me it was a kitten. Eye-opening.

Days pass slowly. Occasionally the weight makes a return, just not in the way it did before. It appears when I travel to more densely populated areas near my home, like an invisible wall warning me to the mindset that permeates the nearby ethers. Now, I take its presence as a silent alert to shield my energy and pay attention.

Sometimes pressure still squeezes tender bronchioles upon entering stores, and they mildly struggle to fill with air. When upsurges in global panic peak, the heaviness rides in on the waves of mass fear and doubt, washing over me at the most unexpected times. Vigilance, presence, and lighter thoughts become constant guardians, stationing at doors and windows like knightly lanterns to keep unwanted shadows at bay.

One such upsurge sneaks in as my sleepy eyes fight against the bright early dawn. Being half-asleep doesn't dim its onslaught, which blows in with tremendous force. Grabbing all my attention, a jagged tug from the unseen, it rips at the flowered comforter that protects me from the morning's cold. This energy doesn't register as oppressive weight but something altogether different. *Death.* Not death as a concept, but the sense of its frigid bony fingers hungrily clawing, tearing at skin and flesh.

It's a distressing feeling to someone who thought they made peace with passing away and the afterlife. That's not to say the thought of leaving my children without a mother is a peaceful one, but this fear feels somewhat foreign at this point in my life. Still, it's fully upon me. So I allow the wave to surface, feeling all that it wants to show me, as pained and twisted panic stomps violently in the center of my solar plexus and sobs of grief, too powerful to hold, rise out of my throat. When tears recede, so does the terror, leaving as quickly as it came.

Questions, now, sit in rows like the large black crows outside my window squawking on a thick dark wire. *What? Why? How? From where?*

It's definite answers I seek. I want to know without a doubt, to touch them. By now, I shouldn't doubt my clarity, but...you know. So, to combat this burning skepticism, I return to the feeling deep within me, the one that says this was not mine, one stamped with mass consciousness fear and COVID fatality. I just can't seem to shake how it feels born of my flesh and bone. Something in me, however, knows otherwise, and I do my best to rest in this, at least.

It's Saturday evening, March 22, to be exact. Tonight, I intend to join a synchronized global meditation to lift the world's consciousness and send healing. First, readying for the event, I join with the Stillness, connecting with Source and all those invited into my circle of influence. Then, shifting my attention, I reach out in awareness and connect with those attending across the world – a heartfelt opening of love and compassion that occurs naturally with a unified desire to extend healing energy.

Energies and visions simultaneously emerge in my mind's eye: a beautiful green-and-blue sphere, marbled in white jet-stream swirls, spinning in a cosmic sea of ink and stars BUT polluted by a viscous, sickly-green ring that ominously surrounds it, blindsiding me with familiar energy. *That blasted elephant, again!* It charged out of the ether's underbrush to make another weight-crushing onslaught, and once more, *I cannot breathe!*

Because the pressure and oppression are instant, I begin to question its return, thinking I'm hallucinating. Suddenly, something in me abruptly stops. *No, I need to shift this now!*

Realizing a change in focus is paramount, I quickly ask to see Mother Earth in Her truth, the Spirit form of Her, whole and pure. As swiftly as it arrived, the ghastly green cloud transforms. In its place, a light – the energy of earth's Spirit – radiates in beautiful gold and translucent white tones, a luminous orb of love to replace images of etheric energy and form. Buoyancy and peace fill the space AND...a dissolution of the pachyderm! No more weight! No more pressure! My full breath returns to lungs that welcome the relief.

In one powerful flash, unmistakable clarity and awareness leave an indelible mark on my heart and mind. I know, without a doubt, in one immediate change of consciousness, the cause of my discomfort – unintentional attunement to lower astral vibrations. The understanding settles on me like penetrating rays of sun, potent enough to shine away any doubt.

The call to "see" with Spiritual Vision, with the sight of Self, could not be more crucial.

For an empath or energy sensitive, vigilance is our watchful parent, guarding loved ones against the wake of negative influences. For years, being mindful of energies has served an important part in navigating my days. Through these challenging times, vigilance has become undeniably essential. My colossal shortness of breath serves as an important reminder.

Energetic shielding, elevation of thoughts and feelings, and soul cleansing, as well as auric and physical space purification, stay in the forefront of my mind. So, while the depth of negativity remains in the mass consciousness, I must do my part to identify any residual issues and continually rise above the energy to function and help others do the healing work on their path.

Time continues to march slowly in quarantine; the second hand's soft monotone ticks like chilled molasses. As hours and days drone on, the weeks shockingly escape me.

Being a social introvert has its plusses and minuses during forced isolation. On the one hand, it's a welcome break from people-y chit-chat and COVID stories. But on the other hand, having a restricted amount of social interaction is enough irritant to counter-balance the upside. So, I intentionally let go of control and use the time to read, study, catch up on copious amounts of outdated TV shows, do crafts, and process what this experience is bringing to the surface. So many lessons, so much time.

It's an early Tuesday morning, just before five o'clock April 7, and I cannot sleep. Typically, this kind of restless-ness means someone unseen knocks on the veil's thin door, offering messages and lessons from the other side. This visit, I find myself unable to ignore the words rattl-ing around in my head. They arrive from a semi-coherent state where the speaker appears with the essence of Mary Queen of Scots (perhaps from a late Netflix session or as a Guide from my lifetime as royalty. Lord knows, I'll take all the help I can get.).

As I lie in bed clinging to sleep, words still tumbling, the urge to write wins out, so I scramble in the dark for pen and paper to keep some remnant of the night with me. As I prop myself up against layers of pillows, the inky blackness swallows me whole. Feeling my way along the steel coils of my notebook, I mark a spot with my index finger and write as I listen to the voice speak.

Through three pages filled with chicken scratch, Spirit impresses upon me the understanding of many challenges. Particularly, a call to "beware or better...BE AWARE, for those we judge today may be gone tomorrow. And when their passing comes, any judgments we issue will be followed with a feeling of guilt."

How I long for the time with Spirit to linger, but the message ends. It's really late or incredibly early, depending on how you want to see it. Tired but still restless, I drop my notebook to the floor, recognizing that sleep is all but gone. Instead, meditation takes its place. As my consciousness lifts, a sudden and overwhelming presence fills my bedroom. Helpers, angels, and passed-over family crowd the space. They stand near me and sit on the bed, giving the room a sense of tender fullness. Saturated with compassion and love so palpable and heartfelt, I feel overcome by their sweetness, so much so that I weep and listen to their reassurance of support, guidance, and urging to keep marching on. The profound feeling of how this pandemic will touch each of us presses again on every particle of my awareness, the profoundly personal way it will affect humanity married with the opportunity to embrace our time now with courage, love, joy, and forgiveness.

With their encouragement to rest, I sink under the heavy covers. A hand from one of my teachers sits etherically on my somnolent head while I drift into the dark to escape the approaching dawn. Their hauntingly beautiful velvet energy gently rocks me into a comforting sleep.

It's late morning, and I cannot escape the bright sun squeezing through closed curtains. Remnants of all that transpired just a few short hours prior linger, and with them a pull to decipher the message of my early morning caller.

Scribbled words messily dance across my notebook. "Read me," they echo. I do recall part of the message, but like all inspired writing, much of it hovers at a level beyond conscious thinking.

Line by line, I transcribe the message. It's long and taken word for word, as channeled information is meant to be. At times the writing sits stacked like delicious pancakes waiting to be hungrily consumed. That's what writing in the dark does, I suppose. A few words, I must omit. Sweet treats or not, the tangle of letters defies decoding, but even without them, the message remains clear:

"Let us stand tall in the face of adversity. The tidal wave is coming. We cannot stop it, but we can choose how we deal with it.

Let us hold one another up in support not judgment. Now and in the days to come, judgment may be our personal downfall. Instead, let what stands before us to call us into action, to let the size of our hearts reign with generosity, to let joy stand beside strength. The fate of humanity rests in the balance... [Can't read a tangle here.]

Perfect health is your birthright. Let the only death be the falling away of personality that judges neighbors and friends. Yes, people will pass on from this physical world. You will miss them...mourn them. Let your memories serve as a reminder that love is neuer, euer lost nor comes with a price because all things come into balance. Learn from them (people and experiences) and learn well; let this time be marked by loue not fear, generosity of spirit, faith in one another, and the belief in life euerlasting.

Haue the courage to let the parts of yourself go that don't serue your highest good and rise up into the Truth of your being. Any negatiuity toward others only has one end and that is toward yourself. Great acts of war, of hatred, are pain in another acted out on those around them. So, be forgiueness, be kindness, and be louing.

Enjoy the simple pleasures – the sun on your face, the wind in your hair, the smile of a stranger. Aboue all else, loue one another and take stock in the good around you. We are indeed blessed, euen if we don't see it. Seek that uision."

~ Peace

I know that the world will never be the same, a feeling that creates a palpable ache on my insides.

This is the grand plan – to awaken us to Truth and Beauty, the sacred energy that lies within everyone and everything.

When we forget, we must choose again and remember.

❖

It's now June and what seems like a lifetime since the COVID epidemic started. To add to the chaos, May 25 brought another epidemic to light – injustice against people of color. After weeks of racial tension, peaceful protests, and race riots, I seek balance and spiritual direction.

These months, marked with much fear, grief, and turmoil, bring questions to the fore: How did we get here, and what are the higher reasons behind the state of the world – the unrest, suffering, and the pandemic? The link is there but still muddy, at least to me.

To answer those questions, we must reflect on manifesting, a state of creating as an inherent quality of our sacred Self. To understand manifesting, we start with the truth that *thoughts are things.* Whatever thoughts we power with emotional energy express in our physical realm as objects, relationships, illness, accidents, or situations built from needs and desires. I'm not talking about "poof" and instant materialization, but the manipulation of energy as a magnetized process of thoughts married with emotions or feelings – the way we draw everything in our life to us. Yes, EVERYTHING – goods sought, "coming down" with a bug, and life events, to name a few. (A concept I've discussed more than once.)

We manifest by employing our God-given energy, creating everything in our life by using the power according to our belief system in one of two ways:

1) In alignment with Source for our highest good;
2) Under the ego's influence of fear.

Our choices (conscious and unconscious) determine the outcome – hidden motives always trumping the overt. The main point is this: where our (mental and emotional) energy goes, life follows. In other words, explore the themes of *any* experience, and behind each, you will find the belief that called it into reality – outside mirroring the inside. Annoying, but highly helpful.

What could this possibly have to do with our current state of the world? I don't think you'll like the answer, but here goes...EVERYTHING.

Let me illuminate by returning to the story at hand.

It's July 6, and for the past week I have been actively seeking peace. Unfortunately, checking small snippets of social media news feeds only serves to aggravate and keep me squarely in conflict on many levels. In an attempt to rise out of a dualistic mindset combined with a desire to see the higher context of all that's happening, I find myself amid a week-long media fast contemplating the intimate relationship between civil unrest, injustice, and the pandemic. Thankfully, my self-imposed famine helped me to leave behind heavy emotions circulating in the ethers and find better understanding.

Since the start of the COVID epidemic, the spiritual reasons behind this disease have regularly pressed on my mind, unfolding into a desire to clearly witness the connection between plagues/pandemics and other global turmoil. As such, tonight I sit comfortably resting in bed as I troll the halls of Google for some three-dimensional information.

For some reason – perhaps Spirit influenced – polio catches my eye. Polio, a significant health bomb in the late 19th century, carried well into the 20th. A virus that attacks the musculoskeletal system, polio impacted thousands between 1896 and the 1980s, leaving many children's bodies contorted, weak, and frequently paralyzed. The virus – largely eradicated by a vaccine first launched in 1953 – still lingered for years in developing countries.

Looking for a social connection to the disease in the U.S. by scrolling through events around polio's early manifestation, I discover a large-scale movement called the Hobo Revolution. During these challenging times, thousands of working-class men took to the roads and railways, "walking" their way across the U.S. looking for work due to an economic collapse. With mass panic resulting in crippled banks, the government froze – no relief efforts existed to help the plethora of people caught in the wake – and Hobos were born. Imagine the feeling of powerlessness across the U.S., the fear of lack due to a crumbling economic foundation, combined with the futile attempt to "move forward" (walking/moving across the U.S. and desperately looking for work/a future under ghost-like government systems).

How does this align with polio? I ask myself. Polio, metaphysically speaking, symbolizes the *belief in powerlessness* (as do all viruses), manifesting in an absence of *strength, coordination, or structure to move forward in life.* Polio, by and large, infected children under the age of five, which symbolizes *joy, youthfulness, and our future selves.* Can you hear/see the alignment of the Hobo movement (difficulty moving forward with life, no support/economic foundation, fear of the future, etc.) with the polio epidemic, one mirroring the other?

Interestingly, evidence suggests that most pandemics across our timeline erupted around wars, struggles for power, civil unrest, and economic disaster. Are you surprised? I'm not.

A feeling of satisfaction washes over me while I quietly rest in a shroud of free-flowing contemplation; this late-night exploration bore juicy fruit. Curiosity with and confirmation by the polio-Hobo connection urge me forward, so I ask silently to whatever guide, angel, or part of my Higher Self listens: *What about COVID and the race revolution now?* Sudden and unmistakable knowing floods in, accompanied by an image and feelings that converge into awareness. In my mind's eye, a vision: George Floyd's face with the caption, "I can't breathe."[53] Immediately, the connection between our "no breath" bug and "no breath" suppressive systems/attitudes align with such clarity, I need to pause and check my pants.

Present-day race revolution distilled into spiritual understanding: Oppression stamps out the very breath in our sisters and brothers of color. "I can't breathe" was George Floyd's cry for mercy, a cry from a man who came to represent a culture suffering widespread injustice. Tragically and unconsciously, yet spiritually, he presented the world with a tremendous opportunity – a wake-up call for change. This opportunity's harbinger: COVID-19, a virus that manifests primarily via lung dysfunction.

---

[53] George Floyd, a 46-year-old African-American man, died on May 25 2020 after being handcuffed and pinned to the ground by a white police officer's knee, an encounter captured on video. The horrific event incited large protests on police brutality and systemic racism in Minneapolis and in more than 150 American cities in the weeks and months that followed. The New York Times, *How George Floyd Died and What Happened Next,"* May 25, 2021, nytimes.com/article/george-floyd.

Lung issues hold the symbolism of *"can't breathe"* – *unable to take in the Breath of Life, and/or the feeling that we don't have a right to take in life.* The result, of which, is *powerful grief.* (Grief, in general, expresses through lung issues.) As I said before, being a virus, it adds the belief in *a lack of power.*

While you chew on that parallel, let me remind you of the message from Spirit, early April. It brings new meaning to urgings of non-judgment, love, and acceptance:

...Let us hold one another up in support not judgment. Now and in the days to come, judgment may be our personal downfall. Instead, let what stands before us to call us into action, to let the size of our hearts reign with generosity, to let joy stand beside strength. The fate of humanity rests in the balance. ...Any negativity toward others only has one end and that is toward yourself. Great acts of war, of hatred, are pain in another acted out on those around them. So, be forgiveness, be kindness, and be loving...

We have manifested an environment of our own making, where oppression has taken a front seat in the grand theatre of life. Of course, oppression is not a new theme. The question is...when will we, as a collective, decide to change it?

A deep and abiding feeling lingers in my awareness: COVID-19 or a similar virus will remain until we transform all systemic and attitudinal oppression into a balance of right action, justice, and love for all and across every system – social, family, cultural, and governmental. This understanding calls forth a potent layer of sadness and regret that blends with dedication, faith, and clarity, the knowing that *I can only do my own work.* Thankfully, personal metamorphosis, no matter how small, is like a pebble in a pond. Its energy ripples out into the world, touching everyone and everything in its wake. We do this by being the light – shining our innate Love and Grace.

As a new dawn breaks, I finish some written reflections on last night's discoveries. The essence lingers as I sit on my patio. Here I'm called to meditate while the sun filters in, points of light through bright green leaves warming my back and decorating the mottled brick patio. That's when I feel spirit again, first as a thought and then a presence. Bob Marley warmly rests an etheric hand on my shoulder. His smile could light a thousand rooms; the potency of his kindness, humor, and love lifts me.

I'm uncertain who drew who, but for days his *Redemption Song* looped in my mind – musical food to help me with my fast and all that's been swirling internally. One phrase echoes on repeat:

> "Emancipate yourself from mental slavery.
> None but ourselves can free our minds."

It's tempting to question what I feel, beginning with... *Really? Why me?* I stop abruptly, however, and resist any further thoughts trying to deny my experience.

All I've learned and felt remains squarely in my heart, a jewel of wisdom and love never to be vanquished.

Remember, we all can manifest change, new attitudes, and a loving world. We all have the power of transformation within us; it rides on the wings of acceptance and becomes grounded through a firmly rooted awareness of Source within all things – all things, all people, and even all challenges before us. For where is God truly absent? Nowhere.

As I finish this chapter in April 2021, COVID and racial unrest still occupy our world. There is much work to be done, and we all have our part.

My hope for you, dear friend, is that you're learning amazing lessons through all that's transpired and in whatever continues to unfold for you. All of life is about learning until we know and live the magnificence of our radiant Self – being and pure expression – moment by moment.

To your Beauty, Love, Joy, and a wonderful world of peace!

Reflections

- *How did the quarantine and events born of COVID-19 change your life?*

- *What was challenging about it for you?*

- *What could you embrace as a blessing?*

- *If the events/situations still seem negative, what silver lining might help change your mind and take in all it had to offer?*

- *How have racial relations and oppression touched your life? What will you do to send love, be more compassionate, or be non-judgmental?*

- *How can you personally create a more inclusive, loving world?*

Epilogue

*The reality of things is hidden
in the realm of the unseen.*
~ Hamza Yusuf

I hope you enjoyed your journey through *The Witch's Cloak: A Memoir of the Unseen* as much as I enjoyed bringing it to you. This project offered many personal opportunities – a time to relive important points of my growth and reflect with warm recognition, remembering that development and evolution is ongoing. That process, like this book, is winding, mystical, and non-linear...and oh, so worthwhile!

Life holds many gifts and blessings if we are willing to look and listen to what the Universe whispers in our ear or places on our lap. Some of our most profound moments happen in the tiny daily miracles and seconds of stillness, times when we least expect them.

Here's to your evolution and life with the unseen.

❀❅❀ Onward and upward!

The breeze at dawn has secrets to tell you.
Don't go back to sleep.
You must ask for what you really want.
Don't go back to sleep.
People are going back and forth across
the doorsill where the two worlds touch.
The door is round and open.
Don't go back to sleep.

~ Rumi

An Empath's Checklist

The intuitive mind is a sacred gift
and the rational mind is a faithful servant.
We have created a society
that honors the servant
and has forgotten the gift.
~ Albert Einstein

The following is a list of talents, qualities, or curses (depending on how you see them). This is the life of empaths or energy sensitives. As particular abilities or traits, what anyone experiences may range in intensity and frequency from person to person and situation to situation.

To use this section as a guide for determining your empathic nature, do the following:

1) Take each trait outlined on the next page and list (on a scale of 1-10) the frequency and/or intensity of your experience with it.

2) When you're finished, add all the numbers to get a total.

3) Divide that total by the number 16.

4) Now, multiply that number by 10, to represent a percentage of intensity with which your sensitivity registers.

Example: 121 (total score) ÷ 16 = 8.06 x 10 = 80.6%

Remember, we often remain unaware of our particular abilities, especially when they operate like breathing – a natural, unconscious, and innate part of moment-by-moment living. So, if your percentage is lower than anticipated, spend a few weeks observing yourself to get more clarity on how you interact with your world.

Empathic Traits

129 /16 = 80

Empaths often can:

10 ❖ Feel another's mood and may experience it as their own;

10 ❖ Become impacted or overwhelmed by another's energy;

10 ❖ Find that watching bloody, violent, or conflict-laden movies, shows, and news feel overwhelming, heart-wrenching, or unbearable;

5 ❖ Sense another's body pain or discomfort and may experience it as their own;

10 ❖ Feel moved to help and/or provide healing to others;

- Have an increased need for baths, showers, and cleaning or washing as a conscious or unconscious need to remove psychic dirt; 8

- Become "rescuers" because other people's pain (mental, emotional, physical) feels like theirs; 10

- Find another's crying very difficult to witness and/or may be easily moved to tears; 10

- Experience vivid dreams filled with graphic, multi-sensory details; 7

- Repeatedly replay the day's events in their minds and relive scenes from life, movies, books, dreams, and especially, experiences that impact them emotionally; 10

- Have difficulty setting boundaries; 10

- Feel more comfortable in black (cloaking) or white (shielding and neutral) clothing as they subconsciously attempt to manage the overwhelming nature of people, crowds, or highly populated areas; 3

- Feel physically drained or a general malaise when around groups; 8

- Know about people, events, etc. without knowing how or why they know; 5

- See or feel the energy of angels, guides, and passed-over entities (people and animals); and 8

- Sense the energy of a house, room, or location but may not be able to articulate or understand their feelings.[54]

For guidance and tools on dealing with empathic stress and navigating the world as a highly sensitive person, please explore *The Soul-Discovery Journalbook: Volume III.* You can also visit this author's website for sessions and workshops. See www.pathways2innerpeace.com.

---

[54]Adriene Nicastro, *The Soul-Discovery Journalbook: An Intimate Journey into Self*, Volume III, (Bellefonte, PA: Pathways to Freedom Press, 2021), pp. 222-223.

Glossary

Abstract mind – the energy of pure knowingness fed by our Higher Self in tune with Source.

Akashic records – the collective energy (vibrational field) of the soul memories of all beings. (See **Soul, Soul Memory**.)

All-That-Is, Divinity, Divine Source, Source, Mother-Father God, God, Universal Power, Cosmic Energy – these terms all refer to the same creative force of the Universe that knows all and feels all; a source of our own Divine Nature and the God within; we are an individualized aspect of this energy, lovingly contained within and intimately connected to Him/Her/It.

Alter ego – the most negative aspect of our personality and ego that holds hostile, aggressive, violent, selfish, and shameful or guilt-producing desires.

Angels – individualized vibrations of pure Divine Energy who never forget or become misaligned with Source; we each have 443,000 angels at our disposal to help, guide, soothe, and heal; their purpose, specific to the angel, is to help us spiritually grow and evolve.

Astral plane – a dimension that all living things pass into as they leave their physical body; the realm of emotions where our Spirit travels when we sleep; the vibration our consciousness visits when we daydream, imagine, dream, or do guided meditation.

Astrology – the ancient study of planetary influences on earthly existence.

Aura – the energy field emanating from all things; holds our physical health, thoughts, attitudes, feelings, emotions, unresolved issues, and beliefs.

Awareness – a state of knowingness beyond what may be identified by concrete mind; a deep feeling that surpasses the lower vibration of words, images, or other logical thoughts and reaches into our Divine Nature and Union with Source.

Chakras – seven energy centers that attach from the etheric body into the physical, linking our form to the mental, emotional, and spiritual bodies; these are ordered from one to seven as follows: root, sacral, solar plexus, heart, throat, third eye, and crown chakras.

Christ – the unconditional love aspect of Source; the highest aspect of our emotional body, which is our Feeling Nature; an energy we all have as Children of God, often labeled as Son, or Son of God; the collective energy of the Christ is all of creation in Unity with Source as the Sonship; frequently thought of as Jesus Christ, the man who attained Christ Consciousness.

Christ Consciousness – the knowingness that all aspects of creation are part of and connected to Source; the recognition of God/Source/Universal Power in all things.

Concrete mind – the aspect of our thinking consumed with planning, logic, figuring, and thoughts regarding our daily earth life; works in conjunction with our ego.

Conscious mind – the part of our psyche as thoughts, drives, and feelings that we are aware of.

Consciousness – an internal state that addresses where our thoughts and emotions lie at any given moment.

Contagion – a mass consciousness belief related to colds and the flu, based on the idea of becoming sick at certain times of the year or for a particular frequency; if we belief we will catch something, that mindset and any related unconscious though processes are dominant, especially over our conscious beliefs.

Discernment – the employment of higher perception without the assessment of ego thinking and beyond the vision of what we see as appearances with our physical eyes; a bridge from higher consciousness to awareness.

Divine Helpers – angels, our Higher Self, and those who have passed over as guides and friends/family in spirit who provide guidance, assistance, encouragement, support, and love.

Ego – the vibration of fear created by us to sound the alarm bells for danger; works with our lower vibrational thoughts through judgment to facilitate separation and lack of love; an operative energy of our personality that uses our soul memory to block us from knowing our Divinity.

Emotional body – a range of esoteric energies from the purity of feelings (Feeling Nature) through the lower energies of emotions; the higher aspect of our emotional body intermingles with our mental body.

Empath – a person who is more intensely affected by energy and thereby absorbs it, wears it, or expresses the energy of those in direct proximity and/or what's held in the ethers.

Etheric – the energy beyond the physical plane that carries our planet's collective consciousness from Earth and all that exists on her.

Etheric body – an exact replica of our physical form; serves as a bridge from the physical to our mental, emotional, and spiritual bodies.

Feeling Nature – The aspect of us that is the high vibration of unconditional love and our pure feelings of our God-self; our third chakra is the entry point of this information.

Feminine energy – the nurturing and sustaining energy of all beings regardless of gender, reflecting one aspect of the whole of our Divine creative flow within; feminine energy gives masculine energy direction and purpose for manifesting and creating.

Guides – entities who previously incarnated on the earth plane; we draw them to us depending on *our* energy, which changes as we grow; attracted based on the path we travel and where our consciousness and evolvement lies, our guides' consciousness is reflective of our own.

Higher Self – our True Nature; the Divine energy within each of us accessed through stillness and connection to our Holy Nature.

Holy Spirit – the action arm of Source in us that bridges our Christ (Self) with our soul; an integral part of us as a transformative power that knows the limitations we believe and the Truth of our being; the Divine energy of comfort and peace.

Inner child – an aspect of personality held in place energetically by our childhood experiences; the appearance of more than one inner child represents fractures of the collective energy of our childhood/adolescence; an inner child appears at a particular age due to childhood events and the child's accompanying perceptions.

Intentions – the powerful combination of thoughts powered by emotions; the directing conscious and subconscious energy behind all we manifest in our life; intentions that are subconscious are always more powerful because they operate often beyond our awareness.

Intuition – the energy of knowing without knowing how or why we know as an aspect of our Divine energy; intuition pours from our solar plexus, helping to give rise to gut feelings and an impression of something beyond our five senses.

Judgment – the energy of fear perpetuated by our ego that separates us from others and Source; the conscious or subconscious evaluation of self or others as right, wrong, good, and/or bad instead of understanding/witnessing their wholeness; seeing without the vision of the Higher Self in a state of unbalance.

Karma – the lower aspect of the Law of Cause and Effect; karma is created when we feel we must pay back, balance, seek revenge, etc. on deeds done to us or those we do unto others; karma is an act of balancing and rebalancing driven by guilt or revenge.

Law of Attraction – like attracts like; positive attracts positive energy; negative attracts negative energy.

Law of Cause and Effect – what goes around comes around; the lowest aspect of this law is karma.

Law of Polarity – all things have an opposite on all energetic levels; to work with this law is to remain in balance.

Magic – the manipulation of energy.

Manifest/Manifesting – exercising our creative abilities to bring into the physical plane that which we want or desire; this includes objects, events, experiences, and situations; the sustaining of energy through our thoughts and feelings in order to bring objects, events, and circumstances into existence; the generation of action energy (**masculine energy**) that is nurtured and sustained (**feminine energy**) long enough to create in the physical plane.

Masculine energy – the energy of action, doing, and initiative; everyone contains masculine energy regardless of gender, as it reflects one aspect of the whole of our Divine creative flow within; feeds feminine energy, offering what may be sustained for what we desire to manifest.

Medium – a person who can do psychic work as well as communicate with spirit, those passed, angels, guides, and or teachers by matching their vibration to the entity that is the focus of their connection; see **psychic.**

Mental body – a spectrum of vibrational energy ranging from concrete mind to abstract mind; intermingles with the higher aspect of our emotional body.

Metaphysical – known, experienced, or existing beyond the realm of physical form through our typical five senses.

Mindfulness – the practice of maintaining a non-judgmental state of heightened or complete awareness of one's thoughts, emotions, or experiences on a moment-to-moment basis.

Non-judgment – the practice of not? evaluating situations, events, objects, or people as good or bad, right or wrong, etc.; releasing the thinking influenced by ego to move beyond duality toward wholeness.

Observing – the act of watching our thoughts, emotions, feelings, beliefs, or attitudes in order to be able to step beyond the influence of ego and personality trends and align with our Higher Self. (See **Witnessing**.)

Oneness – our natural state as a Child of the Divine; the expression of Union with all of life through the collective energy of Intelligent Force/God/Source.

Past lives – previous incarnations of ourselves who appear to have occurred in a time continuum of dates earlier than the perceived present moment; we all have many past lives where an aspect of our Spirit incarnated to learn, grow, and help us return Home.

Psychic – the ability to know beyond the five senses about people, places, events of the past, present, or future; psychic abilities are part of our nature, reading the energy that things, events, and entities express through the magnetized field call the aura.

Psycho-spiritual – the blending of psychological and spiritual transformative experiences and interventions to create that which is both psychological and spiritual, but a distinctly different experience greater than the sum of its two parts.

Reincarnation – the recycling aspect of life by which a portion of any Spirit decides to return to the earth plane to learn and evolve in consciousness; reincarnation occurs with humans, plants, and animals, but only within the species.

Repetition compulsion – a term coined by Sigmund Freud to explain the tendency to repeat past behavior and relive disturbing experiences through real-time events, fantasies, and or dreams. The purpose of this compulsion is an attempt to master subconscious relational challenges and traumatic events.

Soul – an energetic recording device that logs thoughts, feelings, emotions, body sensations, experiences, events, situations, and dreams in our life from the beginning of time to the present and into the future; the soul knows the Truth of our being as well as the misperceptions and illusionary aspects of our consciousness. (See **Akashic records**.)

Soul knot – an energetic tangle in our soul created by our reactions to distressing, traumatic, or problematic situations; current beliefs affect the creating of soul knots, especially when previous events become re-activated by current ones.

Soul memory – the collective information of our entire history held by the soul from the moment of our creation out into our future. (See **Soul**.)

Spirit – the pure aspect of a life created by Source, imbued with the same creative, joy-filled, loving, knowingness as

Source/Mother-Father God; this includes humans, animals, plant life, and minerals.

Spiritual Energetic Protection – the formation of an energetic shield through loving thoughts and feelings, angelic help, and a barrier created in our mind that buffers us from negative energy.

Spirituality – an individual's experience of connection with that power, energy, and love that is Source as Source knows us to be in truth.

Third eye – the energy center of the sixth chakra that allows us to attain higher vision; psychic images often unfold in this space and can be witnessed by focusing with closed eyes on the bridge of our nose that sits between our eyes.

Unconscious mind – part of our psyche that remains hidden from us; it is often filled with trauma, generational belief systems, the parts of us that we don't want to express, and unacceptable thoughts/feelings.

Unseen – energies that include thought-forms, passed over loved ones, spirit guides, spirit teachers, Source, intuition, psychic information, synchronicity, etc.; all vibrations beyond our three-dimensional world not witnessed through our typical five senses.

Veil – an appearance of separation between the earth plane or physical plane and all other planes of existence, which include the etheric, astral, and higher spiritual dimensions; disincarnate spirits exist across the veil, typically in the astral plane, having discarded their physical form.

Witch's knot – a pagan symbol of protection, represented within these pages by ❖.

Witnessing – the act of paying attention to our internal experiences in regards to situations or events; watching how we feel and think about anything in our life in order to move from a state of discomfort to healing; when employed as a mindfulness practice, it involves non-judgment and the movement past the influences of our ego. (See **Observing**.)

Resources

Resources below include books on spirituality, psycho-spirituality, psychology, and metaphysical topics. While this list is far from complete, it includes rich sources to continue and enhance your evolution and discoveries.

Other Books by Adriene Nicastro –

The Soul-Discovery Journalbook: An Intimate Journey into Self, Volume I: A Single Step; Volume II: Constant Companions; Volume III: Metaphysical Musings; Volume IV: A Deeper Gaze; and Volume V: Hip Boots and Waders (paperback)

The Soul-Discovery Journalbook: An Intimate Journey into Self, Volumes I – V (combined volume hardback and eBook)

Little Gifts: The Adventures of a Pigeon Angel (with Peter Santos)

Precious Little Loves

Sacred Garden Fellowship (SGF) – a non-denominational spiritual community dedicated to offering and disseminating teachings from Ascended Masters through the late deep trance channel Rev. Penny Donovan, who taught,

channeled, and facilitated retreats with Don Gilbert until her death in 2020. She is this author's most cherished teacher. Adriene is humbly grateful for Penny's dedication, wisdom, and support throughout the time she studied with her and SGF. Penny has left us a rich legacy and wealth of material that totals over 400 lectures.

Visit www.sacredgardenfellowship.org. or Amazon for more information or publications.

Other Channeled Teachings –

A Course in Miracles: Original Ed., H. Schucman
A Course of Love: Combined Text, M. Perron
The Pathwork of Self-Transformation, E. Pierrakos

Additional Spiritual and Metaphysical Sources –

A New Earth: Awakening to Your Life's Purpose, E. Tolle
The Life and Teaching of the Masters of the Far East, B.T. Spalding
The Art of Forgiveness, Lovingkindness, and Peace, Jack Kornfield
The Art of Spiritual Healing, Joel Goldsmith
Practicing the Presence, Joel Goldsmith
The Four Agreements, Miguel Ruiz
Heal Your Body, Louise Hay
Through Time into Healing, Brian Weiss, MD
The True Power of Water, Masaru Emoto
The Energy Healing Experiments, Gary Schwartz, Ph.D.

About

Adriene Nicastro is an intuitive, psycho-spiritual therapist, ordained minister, healer, teacher, and award-winning author. Through a blend of psycho-spiritual techniques, metaphysical teachings, and spiritual energy healing, she guides individuals and groups through deep levels of holistic transformation.

See www.pathways2innerpeace.com.